by

how2become

A Holiday Rep

Orders: Please contact How2become Ltd, Suite 2, 50 Ch   h
Square Business Centre, Kings Hill, Kent ME19 4YU. Telep   n
(44) 0845 643 1299 – Lines are open Monday to Friday 9ar
5pm. Fax: (44) 01732 525965. You can also order via the   n
address info@how2become.co.uk

ISBN: 9781909229853

First published 2013

Copyright © 2013 How2become Ltd.

Typeset for How2become Ltd by Molly Hill, Canada.

Printed in Great Britain for How2become Ltd by: CMP (uk) Limited,
Poole, Dorset.

CONTENTS

how2become

Dear Sir/Madam,

Thank you very much for purchasing this guide – we value your custom.

The job of a holiday rep member is fantastic; simple as that! Of course, there are difficult times, as there are with all jobs which are 'customer' focused, but the rewards are certainly worth it.

That is why there are so many people, women and men, who want to become a holiday rep. Armed with this guide you will be able to easily pass the selection process for becoming a holiday rep with your chosen tour operator.

As with any job of this nature, there comes a difficult selection process and the smallest mistake can result in failure. Don't leave it to chance that you will be successful. Do everything in your power to prepare and you will find that your confidence will grow and subsequently your chances of success will increase.

Whilst you will need to work hard to pass the selection process, by investing in this guide you have taken a vital step forward in securing your dream job of becoming a holiday rep.

Work hard, never give up, and be what you want.

Kind regards

The How2become Team
www.How2Become.com

A FEW THINGS YOU NEED TO KNOW

The career of a holiday rep is considered, by many, to be a highly rewarding one and therefore it has a highly competitive selection process. Nevertheless, there is a down side which you are probably aware of but you need to know this before you apply.

You will, for the majority of time, be living out of a suitcase and working long hours. You will also find that you'll be away from loved ones for long periods of time, dependant on the tour operator you want to work for.

Are you prepared to be away from friends, family and partner for week upon week? Are you prepared for working unsociable hours and eating when you are supposed to be sleeping, and sleeping when you should be eating? These are all things that you need to consider and be aware of before applying.

You'll no doubt be asked questions about the negative aspects of the job during the selection interview. Therefore, you need to be aware of what the negative aspects are, but more importantly, how to convince the panel that they are not a problem for you.

Within this guide we will show you exactly how to do this and how to answer all of your questions in a positive and confident manner.

CHAPTER ONE

INTRODUCTION

Below, we have provided a list and description of the different types of holiday reps and the work their roles involve. This section is designed to give you a better understanding of the rep you might want to become. What you will notice from the section below is that a number of the positions overlap in terms of job description and responsibilities and when you arrive at your resort you will often be working with a number of the different types of rep. What ever rep you decide to become, this guide will help you through the application process.

THE DIFFERENT TYPES OF HOLIDAY REPS

Overseas/Holiday Reps
Holiday reps are also known as Customer Services Rep, Resort Rep and Overseas Rep depending on the tour

operator you work for, but they all basically have the same role. To be a successful overseas rep you must be outgoing, enjoy meeting and interacting with new people and embrace new experiences and cultures. It is also important that you have excellent sales skills as well as possessing an energetic approach to your work, as it can be a very busy at times. The role will often include meeting customers at the airport, presenting them with information that is useful and accurate, holding welcoming meetings, visiting hotels on a regular basis to offer guidance and support, displaying high levels of customer service and resolving any problems in a calm and collective manner. Other aspects of the job include guiding excursions, carrying out health and safety checks on the hotel(s) and completion of paperwork.

Club Reps

There are many different names for this type of rep; young person's rep, Club 18-30, Escapades Rep, 2wenty's Rep (First Choice), Club Freestyle Rep (Thomson). However, they are all essentially the same role. A young person's rep is a person that ensures that groups of men and women, aged between 18 to 35, have the time of their life on holiday! By applying to become this type of rep you will be sent to the liveliest and busiest resorts. The main responsibilities of a club rep are almost identical to that of a holiday rep. However, in addition to these daily responsibilities they must also organise the evening entertainment such as pool parties, bar/pub crawls, party nights and beach parties. And while your guests are sleeping you will need to be up early to perform your daily responsibilities such as holding welcome events and dealing with customer complaints in addition to the odd hangover!

Entertainment Reps

An entertainment rep is a very demanding role and you will also be expected to join in a wide range of other activities to assist the overseas reps.

During the day, you will be making yourself known to the customers, helping everyone join in the fun and presenting a full and varied programme of family-focused activities. During the night, you will be on centre stage performing a wide variety of shows to provide the evenings entertainment. From performing in West End style productions such as Frankenstein and variety shows, to hosting TV game shows to keep the children entertained. For this role you will ideally have a talent or keen interest in dancing, singing or performing, although it is not essential.

Children's Reps

Children's Reps will often perform a similar role to that of the entertainment rep with their focus mainly on the younger children. They are often in charge of kids clubs providing a welcomed break for parents, while at the same time organising games, challenges and activities for young children in order to ensure they enjoy every minute of their holiday. This role requires a number of key skills. For example, you must enjoy working with children and have the patience to deal with children. Their parents will only want to leave their children in your hands if they feel you are confident and capable in your role.

As this role specifically deals with young children there are often stricter requirements when applying for this role. You should ensure that you check with the tour operator as to what these requirements are. Many will often require at least six months' experience of professional childcare and/or a childcare qualification at NVQ Level 2. Alternatively, you may

be eligible if you hold qualifications such as BTEC National Diploma in Childhood Studies. You will need to check the requirements of the tour company you want to join.

Transfer Rep

A transfer rep is somebody who mainly accompanies holiday makers to and from the airport and hotels. A transfer rep is normally the first person the holiday maker sees to represent the tour company, so they must always be friendly and approachable as they are the face of the company. During the coach trips to the resorts you will be responsible for conducting a welcome talk that includes details of basic information about the resort, which drop offs you will be going to and how long the trip will last plus, most importantly, about when their welcome meeting will be conducted.

Transfer reps must also ensure that the guests are booked in to their accommodation and they are dropped off at the correct resort. In the event that the departure flight is delayed it is the responsibility of the transfer rep to keep the customers informed of any developments. As with the role of overseas rep the transfer rep may also act as a guide on excursions.

Qualifications needed to become a Holiday Rep

The qualifications you will need depend on what kind of position you are seeking. As mentioned above the position of children's rep is one that often requires specific qualifications.

Most reps need to be at least 18 and some positions require you to be 21 years old. Formal qualifications are not generally required for the position of a holiday rep. However, good GCSE grades / A-level grades or any qualification in Travel and Tourism will always help your chances of success. In addition to this, any customer service experience is also

a valuable asset to have as it demonstrates a key skill the recruitment team are looking for. This can even be through a part-time job while you were studying or part of your full-time job that you do on a daily basis. There is also no requirement to speak a different language (although it will help if you do, so make sure you mention it).

THE QUALITIES AND ATTRIBUTES OF HOLIDAY REP

These are extremely important to your role as a holiday rep and the selection panel will be looking closely to see if you have them. Some of the qualities and attributes you will have naturally, but some of them will have to be acquired through practice and self awareness.

Being **DEPENDABLE** is an important asset, especially when working as part of a team. Can the tour operator depend on you to turn up on time, or help out in any situation without being asked to?

Do you take a **PRIDE** in your appearance, **LOOK GOOD** at all times and care about your **PERSONAL HYGIENE**? Paying close attention to these important attributes can be the difference between success and failure.

What are your **COMMUNICATION SKILLS** like and are you an effective **COMMUNICATOR** and **LISTENER**? Are you able to deal with complaints in a **CALM** and **COMPOSED** manner?

Do you have a **SENSE OF HUMOUR** that is relevant and do you have a **CARING ATTITUDE**?

Are you **MATURE** and **ORGANISED** and can you demonstrate these qualities to the selection panel?

We will now provide you with a 'qualities and attributes' check list. We advise that you look at each one carefully and write down, in the spaces provided, a situation where you have recently demonstrated each quality. Keep hold of the checklist as you will need this at a later point within the guide.

THE QUALITIES AND ATTRIBUTES OF HOLIDAY REP

QUALITIES AND ATTRIBUTES CHECKLIST

DEPENDABLE

UNDERSTANDING NATURE

CARING

GOOD SENSE OF HUMOUR

TAKING PRIDE IN MY APPEARANCE

MOTIVATED

ENTHUSIASTIC

CONFIDENT

A FRIENDLY NATURE

RESILIENT

PATIENT

MATURE OUTLOOK

ORGANISED

EFFECTIVE LISTNER

GOOD COMMUNICATOR

YOUR KEY RESPONSBILITIES AS A HOLIDAY REP

Customer Service

- Work to ensure that you consistently deliver an excellent level of service.

- Recognise every customer as an individual.

- You should be the local expert for your customers by providing up-to-date and relevant information of the surrounding areas.

- Obtain feedback from customers after they have been on a company excursion.

- Deal with all customer problems effectively and seeking guidance from Resort Team Manager / Leader where necessary.

- Ensure customer communication is delivered in line with company guidelines.

- Transferring holiday makers to and from the airport and hotel.

Accommodation Health & Safety Checks

- Complete Health and Safety checks and report concerns to Resort Team Manager.

- Report back to your team leader with your suggested improvements. This is key to improving the service you can offer your customers.

- Ensure any issues affecting customer satisfaction are brought to the attention of the Resort Team Manager.

- Work alongside your suppliers to enhance the customers' holiday.

- Be responsible for the customers' hotel reservation ensuring correct room types and extras are delivered as booked.

Conducting welcome meetings/selling excursions

- Provide targeted holiday information, whilst ensuring customers are briefed on the excursions available to them.

- You may have to achieve sales targets through selling excursions, car hire, telephone cards and other new products and services introduced by the company.

- If you are required to sell you will normally have to decide on which product(s) to sell in order to gain maximum sales and customer satisfaction.

- Possess a full understanding of every product and service that you sell to your customers.

- Recommend improvements to the Company excursions from the feedback from your customers

- Guiding your customers on the excursions/ trips you have sold them.

- Collecting and balancing foreign money

Completing paperwork

- Be responsible for the safe keeping of and account for all money collected.

- Complete appropriate forms and reports.

- Meet administrative deadlines.

CHOOSING THE CORRECT TOUR OPERATOR

Each tour operator is a different employer and therefore the quality of career you get from each of them will vary. There is a huge range of tour operators to choose from and you must take your time when considering which one to apply for.

You can apply to a tour operator in a number of different ways. Firstly, you can download an application form from their website; print it off before completing it and sending it to the company. Alternatively, you can fill out an online application.

If you go to the website of the tour operator you wish to apply to join and go down to the bottom of the page, they will often have a link that says "jobs". If you click on this link it will not only tell the jobs the company has available but also how you can apply.

If you cannot find this link or any information about the application process you can either call the tour operator and ask them about the best course of action or email them. See our USEFUL CONTACTS section for more details. Each tour operator will usually have an email address you can email for more information. Failing all these methods you can write to the company and ask them to send you an application form.

Remember that you will probably be working for them for a long time, so you need to feel comfortable with your employer. Don't get carried away with just wanting to be a holiday rep.

To begin with, you should ask yourself the following questions:

- Why do I want to be a holiday rep?

- What do I expect to get out of my job?

- Do I mind being away from home for long periods of time?

- Is the image of the tour operator important to me?

- Is travelling important to me?

Once you have answered these questions honestly, you will begin to realise the type of tour operator you should approach.

WHY DO I WANT TO BECOME A HOLIDAY REP?

The answer to this question is probably obvious. You want to meet new and exciting people and not to have a boring 9-to-5 job like the majority of people? If these are your reasons for wanting to become a holiday rep, then you have chosen the right career! However, when you are preparing for the selection process you need to change your attitude to what the career of a holiday rep is all about. We will cover this in more detail later, but you need to realise that each tour operator is a business, solely interested in providing a high level of customer service to everyone who stays with them. If they provide an excellent level of service then people are more likely to use them again. This is where you come in! Have you ever travelled with a particular tour operator and had a bad experience with regards to the customer service you received? If you have, would you use with them again? Probably not! Hopefully you are beginning to understand why it is important that each tour operator only employs people who are capable of being a role-model for their organisation and also capable of providing excellent customer service. Start to think like the recruitment staff and focus on the type of people they are looking to recruit – those who are presentable, who are capable of providing a high level of service, are reliable and are totally customer-focused.

WHAT DO I EXPECT TO GET OUT OF MY JOB?

This is another important question you should ask yourself.

The answer you come up with will very much determine the type of tour operator you decide to apply for. Remember that the majority of tour operators do ask if you have a resort that you would prefer to work in. However, it is not always guaranteed that you will get placed there. They will take into consideration factors like speaking the local language and having a good understanding of lots of personal experience of the area. With some companies the holiday reps will typically start in European countries for their first couple of seasons and then have the opportunity to progress to places such as the Caribbean, Asia and America. With others, new holiday representatives can be sent to long-haul destinations on their very first season.

Another factor that you may want to consider when asking this question is what you want to do after your season has finished. Many holiday reps choose to undertake a ski season and then go back out again the following summer. However, some have the opportunity to go back home and work as travel agents in their local towns. All of these factors should be taken into consideration when considering what you want from your job and from your tour operator. Once you have done this, you can then start to take a look at the different types of tour operator that are most suited to your own personal needs.

DO I MIND BEING AWAY FROM HOME FOR LONG PERIODS OF TIME?

Many holiday reps enjoy being away from home for weeks at a time and this is another important question that you

should take seriously. Take a look at your own personal circumstances. Do you have a partner? How would he/she feel about you being away from home for weeks at a time? How would you feel about being away from them?

If you are in the position that you have no ties or commitments, then your choice of work and tour operator will be an easy one. You would find it easier to relocate closer to an airport, if required, without those ties that can potentially hold you back.

How would you respond to an interview question of this nature?

Q. Could you provide examples of when you have been away from home for weeks at a time?

If you progress to the interview stage you are more than likely to be asked a question of this nature. You will need to demonstrate that you have thought long and hard about your choice of career and that you are prepared for the lengthy periods away from home.

IS THE IMAGE OF THE TOUR OPERATOR IMPORTANT TO ME?

Many people are not concerned about the image of the tour operator and are prepared to work for anybody, just to get the job.

Ask yourself how important the image of the tour operator is to you and you will begin to understand the type of tour operator you want to apply for. Whichever one you decide to apply for you will need to spend time studying all there is to know about that particular tour operator. You are almost guaranteed to be asked the question – *'Why do you want to join our tour operator?'*

Within our 'useful contacts' section, we have provided a list of all the UK and

International tour operators' contact details, including their website addresses. When deciding which tour operator to apply for, spend a little time visiting their website and you will begin to get a feel as to what they are about. Also, try asking friends and relatives what they think about the tour operator you are hoping to join. It is worth spending a little bit of time carrying out research on each tour operator, before committing to their selection process.

THE SELECTION PROCESS

The holiday rep selection process is a difficult one to pass. Some candidates will find it harder than others, but the main thing to remember is that preparation and determination are key to your success. Throughout the process you need to have a positive attitude and be confident in your own abilities. Of course, it is quite normal to feel apprehensive and nervous about the whole thing, but believing in yourself is essential. The recruitment staff want to see a person who is confident (but not overconfident), reliable, committed and capable of dealing with difficult situations under pressure.

The selection process has been designed to pick the best people for the job. The panel wants to choose the right people for their tour operator and their customers, which is why we have already told you to learn as much as possible about the one you want to join.

Most of the tour operators have a 3 stage selection process which is detailed as follows.

STAGE ONE

- Initial paper-sift
- The application form

STAGE 2

- Presentation
- Team assessments
- Tests

STAGE 3

- Formal Interview

NOTE: Stages 2 and 3 will normally occur on the same day, stage 2 in the morning and, if you are successful, stage 3 in the afternoon.

A typical assessment day would be as follows:

At the beginning of the day you will be told about the history of the tour operator and what services they offer. Listen carefully to this as what they tell you may come up as test questions later on in the day. You will then be broken into groups depending on the amount of people that have attended. You will then be asked to deliver your two-minute presentation. You then have a problem solving group exercise and it's important at this point to listen to others, but also make sure your views are heard.

You will then have a basic maths test, including percentages and currency converting and also a brochure test. Some tour operators have an English test where you will be required to pick up and correct spelling and grammar mistakes. Finally,

there is a role-play where you will have to act as Rep in a difficult situation. There will normally then be a break and when you come back, you will either be offered a one-to-one interview, or your day will finish there.

Each tour operator's selection process will vary slightly and it is important that you check the process first before planning your own preparation. However, most of them are the same in the fact that you must pass each stage before progressing on to the next one. This means that it is vital you give 100% preparation and commitment to each stage. At each stage you must show the recruitment team that you have the necessary qualities and attributes they are looking for.

Apart from this, you will be required to demonstrate that you are capable of providing a level of customer service that matches their own standards and show that you are dependable and will be able to work effectively in a team environment. Obviously, this is quite a tall order for anyone regardless of their abilities, but if you plan each stage separately and break down each section into manageable portions, you will find it easier to handle.

Within this guide, we have broken down each of the selection areas separately for ease of use. We recommend you use one section at a time, as and when required.

CHAPTER TWO

THE TOP 10 INSIDER TIPS AND ADVICE

TIP 1 – CHOOSE THE RIGHT TOUR OPERATOR

When choosing the tour operator that you want to apply to join you need to carry out as much research as possible before deciding to begin with their application process. You may decide to apply to a number of operators at the same time. While this can be perceived as positive in terms of increasing your chances of success, you must ensure each application is given the preparation it deserves. It can be viewed as being more effective if you apply to a select few first and spend a greater amount of time researching each of them. The more you can make your application *specific* to that particular tour operator the more you will stand out as

the ideal candidate.

By demonstrating at the interview that you have researched their tour operator thoroughly, you show a higher level of commitment and you also demonstrate that you are committed to working with them. The mistake too many people make is that they focus their efforts on just 'becoming a holiday rep', when they should really be focusing their efforts on becoming a holiday rep with 'x tour operator'.

Try to imagine yourself as one of the recruitment staff. You are presented with two candidates to choose from. They have both passed all of the assessments and they would both be good for your company. One has applied for four different tour operators and the other has only applied for just yours. Which one would you choose?

TIP 2 – KNOW HOW TO COMPLETE THE APPLICATION FORM CORRECTLY

Over 96% of candidates fail at the application form stage, usually due to a number of factors. In the majority of cases, candidates fail to demonstrate that they have the right customer service skills to become a holiday rep. That is why it is so important that you take your time when answering these questions and structure your application form responses in an effective manner.

Even if you have no or very little experience of customer service skills, this should not stand in your way. Understanding the importance of customer service and being able to apply it throughout the selection process is far more important. Just because somebody has worked in a customer focused environment for many years, does not automatically mean they are good at providing it.

Before completing your application form read our section entitled 'The application form' for a detailed explanation on how to tackle the questions.

TIP 3 – RESEARCH THE TOUR OPERATOR THOROUGHLY

Many people do not spend enough time researching their chosen tour operator. Then, when it comes to the interview, they fail to answer specific tour operator related questions effectively and end up failing the whole process. You will be asked questions about the tour operator, how it operates, what destinations they fly to and other important facts that you need to know as a holiday rep.

This is no different to any other interview that you attend. The first and most important topic to research is the company and the role you are applying for.

There are a number of places that you can find relevant information about the tour operator you are applying for which we will discuss later on in the guide. Now, try to imagine what it must be like for those people who apply to 4 or 5 tour operators at a time. Can they give sufficient preparation time to each one? Probably not. Within the guide we have provided you with a template that contains all of the areas you should research. Make sure you research them thoroughly.

TIP 4 – EFFECTIVE COMMUNICATION SKILLS

Good communication skills are essential to the role of a holiday rep. Although the job is glamorous it is still customer focused and you will need to demonstrate that you have the ability to communicate effectively at all times. Try to think of

an occasion when somebody has annoyed you. How did you react? Do you have the ability to stay calm in a confrontational situation? Of course, everybody feels uncomfortable when faced with a confrontational person, but it is your ability to defuse these situations that will set you apart from the rest of the candidates.

Effective communication skills can be worked on and during this guide we will provide you with information and exercises to help you improve this important attribute.

TIP 5 – KNOW HOW TO HANDLE COMPLAINTS EFFECTIVELY

It is an unfortunate fact that most holiday reps encounter complaints. Part of the job involves knowing how to deal with them correctly. If a flight is delayed, passengers are far more likely to complain about trivial things when they arrive at their resort, which wouldn't normally bother them.

There are a wide variety of reasons why people complain, but the fact is you need to know how to deal with them effectively and efficiently in order to deliver a high level of customer service. The customer is not concerned with why or how the problem has arisen; all they want to know is how you are going to deal with the issues. It is your ability to perform in situations like these that will set you apart from the rest of the candidates.

TIP 6 – KNOW WHAT TO WEAR FOR YOUR INTERVIEW

You only get one chance to make a first impression. In fact, a first impression is often formed within the first seven seconds of meeting someone!

You should keep this in mind when deciding what to wear to your assessment day and your interview. It is only natural the interview panel will form an opinion of you as soon as they see you, so you will need to create the right impression from the offset.

Whilst you will probably have a good Idea of what to wear, how to apply your make up (if you wear it) and how to present yourself, you should still take the time to re-assess your appearance.

TIP 7 – CREATE AN EFFECTIVE INTRODUCTION

During the actual interview/assessment day you will be required to introduce yourself to the rest of the candidates and the selection staff. This is done for a number of reasons. One of them is to allow the recruitment staff to see how confident you are and how well you present yourself. I addition to these reasons it also acts as an effective ice breaker.

Everybody will be nervous during the interview, that's a fact. But you still need to create a good impression right from the offset. The tour operator recruitment staff will be watching you and assessing your abilities right from the word go.

Tip – If the operator asks the question "who wants to go first?" you can create a great first impression by putting your hand up. This will immediately make the assessment team take note of your confidence and your ability to address a group of people you have only just met, something which is crucial to the role of a holiday rep.

It is important that you write down and practice your introduction beforehand.

Try standing up and saying your prepared introduction in

front of your friends or relatives and you will see how difficult it can be. However, the more times you practice it, the better you will become at putting yourself across in a positive and confident manner.

TIP 8 – UNDERSTAND TEAM WORK

What does the term 'teamwork' actually mean?

Here is a good explanation:

> *'Working as part of a group in which there is a shared goal. In order to achieve this, different members of the team take on different roles.'*

When you are working as holiday rep it is vital that you are capable of working as an effective team member. Your role as a holiday rep will mean you will have to work closely as a team on a daily basis with other reps, restaurant owners, hotel owners and tour guides to deliver the required high level of customer service.

- Are you able to create a rapport with any team you work with?

- Can you bring something valuable to that team?

- Do you make an effort to mix with the team and do you involve others?

During the selection process you will be assessed in a team environment. You may be asked to take part in a group discussion and you'll be monitored in relation to how you react to certain situations and scenarios. Throughout this guide we will show you how to work effectively in a team environment.

TIP 9 – KNOW THE INTERVIEW QUESTIONS

Imagine being told the type of questions that you will be asked prior to going into your interview. We will give you those questions. We have spent hours talking to current serving holiday reps, recruitment staff and applicants who have failed the process in order to obtain as many interview questions as possible.

We have also spent the time researching how to effectively answer those questions, so you don't have to. Read the 'Interview' section of this guide thoroughly, paying particular attention to the sample responses. Then, create your own personal and individual responses to the questions provided based on your own opinions and experiences. This will involve quite a lot of work but it will help you to get in the right frame of mind for the interview.

TIP 10 – FINALLY, DON'T GIVE UP!

Too many people give up at the first attempt.

Yes, it is disheartening when you fail things in life but never give up. There have been many examples of people eventually succeeding at the fifth or sixth attempt. The key is to keep learning and improving your skills.

If you fail something in life, look upon it as an opportunity for improvement.

- Where did you go wrong?

- What can you do next time to improve?

- Did you ask for feedback?

- Can you learn from others?

- Are you prepared to learn from your mistakes?

- If you want something so bad then you can get it.

- Sometimes it takes people years to get where they want to be. But by staying focused, motivated and driven, you can be what you want.

CHAPTER THREE
THE APPLICATION FORM

INTRODUCTION

Around 96% of applicants fail this important stage which is usually due to a lack of preparation.

Each tour operator application form will vary slightly, but within this section we have provided you with insider tips and advice on how to complete it correctly.

Key Tip – If you are submitting your application online make sure you print off your responses before you submit it to the tour operator. If you are submitting an application by post make sure you photocopy it first. The reason for this is that people often forget the responses and information that they put down in their application form, especially with applicants often applying to a number of different tour operators. By taking a copy of it you can read through it the night before

your assessment/interview to remind yourself of exactly what you put in your application.

TIP 1 – READ THE APPLICATION FORM THOROUGHLY FIRST

Before you complete the application form read all of the sections, advice and guidance first, at least twice, to see what is required. For example, at the top of the application form, or within the guidance notes, it may ask for a particular colour of ink. It is surprising how many people fail to follow this simple instruction. If you do not complete the application form as requested then this shows an inability to follow simple instructions – an asset that is vital to the role of a holiday rep.

TIP 2 – PRACTICE FIRST

Make sure you photocopy/print off the application form and practice first. You are certain to make mistakes the first time around, so it is wise to practise and write down your answers before completing your submission. Submitting application forms with an error or spelling mistake creates a bad impression (something which you want to avoid).

The application form may also provide you with boxes in which to complete your responses. Make sure you keep your answers within these boxes, unless specifically instructed otherwise.

TIP 3 – PERSONAL DETAILS

Within the application form it will ask you to complete your personal details. This section is relatively straightforward, but some tour operators ask you to complete it as shown on your passport. Make sure you cross reference your passport and complete the details as shown, if required to do so.

TIP 4 – LANGUAGES

Some application forms will ask you if you speak any foreign languages and if so at what level (from basic to fluent). Make sure that the indication you provide is a true reflection of the level to which you can speak that language. There are two reasons for this, firstly you may be asked about this on the recruitment day and secondly it could influence where you are placed as a rep.

TIP 5 – PERSONAL QUALITIES

Within the application form you will normally be asked to complete a section that relates to your personal qualities and attributes. Remember to be as open and honest as possible as you may be asked about your application form at a later date.

The question may read:

"What qualities do you possess to become a successful Holiday Rep?"

Remember in the 'QUALITIES AND ATTRIBUTES' section we discussed some of these, and how important they are? When answering this section of the application form, it is important to let the recruitment team know you have these skills.

A sample answer to this question might be:

"I am an enthusiastic, loyal and resilient person who takes great pride in my appearance. Having previously worked in a customer-focused environment I fully understand the needs of others and believe my patience is a valuable asset in situations where others require my assistance. I thrive in any team environment and always try to use my excellent communication skills to listen to what others have to say whilst making valuable contributions myself. I have a friendly

and caring personality which enables me to be supportive of my colleagues, and I always treat everybody as an individual"

Now create your own response to this question based on the personal qualities and attributes that you have.

Don't forget to consider the following keywords in your response:

KEY WORDS: Confident, enthusiastic, loyal, resilient, pride in my appearance, customer skills, needs of others, patience, helping others, considerate, team player, team environment, friendly and caring, excellent communication skills, listen, valuable contributions, supportive, capable of working under pressure, sense of humour, organised, mature.

TIP 6 – CUSTOMER SERVICE RESPONSE

Within the application form you may also be asked to complete a section in relation to customer service and where you have demonstrated this in a previous or current role.

The question may be posed in a manner similar to the following:

"Please give details of experienced gained or training received in sales."

Of course, each and every one of us has different work experiences that we can draw from, but this an extremely important section of the application form and it is important that you demonstrate the required qualities here.

The following is an example of the type of response the recruitment team are seeking. Your customer service example is important and it could be the difference between making and not making it through to the next stage.

Make sure you take your time when preparing your response.

Again, take the time to construct your own, individual response but first read our example on the following page.

Customer service response

"Whilst working as a sales representative for my current employer, I received a telephone call from an unhappy customer. Whilst listening to his concerns, I could sense that he was beginning to regret placing an order with our company. Before talking to him about the situation, I tried to realise how stressful it must be for him to be in this situation. I tried to think about what I could do to help reduce his worries and resolve the situation to his satisfaction. I informed him that I fully understood his concerns and I reassured him that I would do everything possible to help him. As soon as I told him this I could sense how thrilled he was to know that I would be helping him. I immediately dispatched another order whilst on the phone to him, making sure that the order would be delivered that same day. I also told him that I would call him later that day to make sure he was happy with the new order. Later that day, I telephoned the gentleman to check everything was to his satisfaction. The sound in his voice was very rewarding and I realised that with just a little help I had made such a difference to his day, making him feel like a valued customer."

Further Customer Service Questions

"Detail all customer service experience which you feel would benefit your application."

Once again, the question relates directly to your customer service experience.

Some tour operators require you to have a minimum of six months experience in a customer-based environment.

This can be any type of customer experience, whether it is working in a shop, hotel, restaurant, or even answering the phone to customers or clients. There now follows a sample response to this type of question.

As a starting point you may find it helpful to write down your customer service experience before actually committing to a response. You'll be surprised at what experience you will have and how it can be adapted to fit the question. Once you have read our example response use a blank sheet of paper to structure your own.

Response Example:

"In my current position as the manager of a restaurant I am required to deliver excellent customer service, which includes the welcoming of customers, dealing with any complaints or queries, managing and leading the team to ensure we exceed the customers' expectations, providing a fast and efficient service and ensuring the team presents a highly professional image that represents the standards set by the restaurant. Prior to my current position, I worked as a customer service representative, responsible for answering calls and dealing with queries and complaints about the service. I was often confronted with dissatisfied customers and part of my role was to defuse confrontational situations and provide a resolution that the customers were happy with. The best part of the job was having the ability to sort out the customers' problems in a satisfactory manner, making them feel that the company genuinely cared about their complaint or query."

FURTHER APPLICATION FORM QUESTIONS

"Having applied for the position of holiday rep, you are obviously interested in travel and people. What other reasons do you have for applying?"

This type of question is designed to assess the reasons why you want to become a holiday rep. When answering questions of this nature avoid talking about the glamorous side of the job or the fact that the image of a holiday rep appeals to you.

Instead you should concentrate on the following areas:

- The reputation the tour operator has (providing it is positive)

- You enjoy working in a challenging role

- The varied roster or shift system

- Working in a customer-based role

- Providing a high level of service

We have now provided a sample response to this type of question. Take the time to read the response before using a blank sheet of paper to construct your own individual response.

Remember to be positive and enthusiastic in your reply.

Response Example:

"I have always had the ambition of becoming a holiday rep from an early age and now that I have the relevant customer service skills I am ready to pursue my ambition. Other reasons for my application include the fact that I enjoy working in a customer-focused environment and thrive on

the challenges that such a career brings. There is no better feeling than successfully resolving issues for customers and I believe I would enjoy the responsibilities that a holiday rep has. I personally set myself high standards and would enjoy working for a tour operator that expects the same from its staff. I love working in a team environment where everybody pulls together to achieve a common goal. I am the type of person who works well under pressure and would feel that the role of a holiday rep would be suited to my qualities and attributes. Finally, after researching the tour operator, I have been impressed by the high level of service it offers and the reputation that it has successfully built so far. I would like to be a part of that team and would work hard to ensure the current standards are maintained."

"Why do you want to work for this tour company? And why should we consider your application?"

The only way that you can effectively answer this question is to research the tour operator.

When answering this type of question try to include any success stories the tour operator might have achieved in recent times. Areas that you should not include in your response relate to leave, salary, uniform, subsidised travel and holidays etc. Focus on the facts about the tour operator and try to demonstrate that you have taken the time to look into the way it operates. Maybe you have used them before and had a good experience with one of their holiday reps?

There now follows a sample response to this type of question. Read it thoroughly before using a blank sheet of paper to construct your own.

Response Example:

"There are a number of reasons why I would like to work for

this company. The first and foremost reason is the reputation the tour operator has. I would like to work for a tour operator that sets high standards and takes a pride in the service it offers, and I would like to be a part of that team. Because the tour operator is continuously improving, it is likely to mean there will be exciting and challenging times ahead, which appeals to me. I have also been impressed by the ongoing development and training that is provided by the tour operator, which would help me to maintain a high standard throughout my career, if I am to be successful. Finally, I recently had the pleasure of travelling with the tour operator whilst on holiday. The holiday reps were exceptional in their professionalism and high level of service, which makes the tour operator an even more appealing one to work for."

"Describe one specific time when you have had to think quickly under pressure in order to address a situation that required immediate action. What prompted you to try that approach and what was the result?"

This type of question has been designed to assess your ability to work quickly under pressure whilst having the confidence to take action when necessary. Try to think of an example when you have had to work quickly under pressure to prevent a situation from deteriorating.

Make sure you give the reasons why you took that particular action and explain the result. You may also wish to say, at the end of your response, what you learned from your experience.

There now follows a sample response to give you some ideas to help you create your own. The response we have provided explains a situation where a member of staff is following a set routine which he/she has been given during training (something you will be required to do as a holiday rep).

It also emphasises the need for ensuring everyone was safe throughout the incident, including an explanation for why it was necessary to remain calm (again, something you will have to do whilst working as a holiday rep).

Response Example:

"Whilst working for my current employer as a shop sales assistant, I was confronted with an emergency situation during a busy Saturday morning. I was stock-taking in the store room which is located on the 3rd floor of the store. Whilst working, I suddenly began to smell a strong burning smell but could not tell where it was coming from. I immediately began to follow the procedures given during my staff induction training and raised the alarm by breaking the alarm call point located at the store room exit. I walked calmly out of the store room, but noticed that all the customers were ignoring the alarm and continuing to shop. I immediately shouted, in a calm but raised voice, for everyone to leave the shop, via the nearest stairway exit, due to an incident. I reemphasised the importance that people should not use the lifts. People began to leave via the stairway and I went over to the till area and called the Fire Brigade before making my way out via the stairs.

On the way down, I calmly informed other members of staff that there was an incident and that we should leave the shop and await the arrival of the Fire Brigade. When we got outside, a roll-call of all members of staff was taken. The Fire Brigade soon arrived and I informed them of the location of the store room and the reason that the alarm had been raised. Following their investigation, it was found that an electrical socket had overheated and was smouldering at the rear of the store room.

The reason that I took this action was that I am required

to follow the training provided during my staff induction. Although I was effectively evacuating the whole of the store and losing the company money, the safety of the customers and other staff members was paramount. I did everything in a calm manner. I needed to remain calm throughout so that the customers would not panic whilst evacuating. If they were to panic, then injury could have occurred whilst they were leaving the shop via the stairs.

The end result was that everybody was accounted for and there were no injuries. Also, the possibility of a major fire was averted because the Fire Brigade were called quickly and were, therefore, able to deal with the fire before it got out of hand."

"Describe one specific time when you had to convey an unpopular decision to an individual or group. How did you approach that person or group? How did you deal with the situation? Was the situation resolved?"

This type of question is designed to assess your ability to deal with difficult situations in an assertive manner. Giving unpopular news or constructive feedback is difficult, even for the most confident of people. When working as a holiday rep you will sometimes be dealing with customers who are rude and confrontational. You will be required to deal with these situations and sometimes give customers unwelcome news.

Being able to do this in an effective manner is quite a skill and the tour operator recruitment staff want to see you have the potential to do this in a real life situation.

There now follows a sample response to this type of question. Read it carefully before structuring your own response using the template provided.

Response Example:

"Whilst working in my current position as a hotel receptionist, I was confronted with a situation where our central reservation booking system had mistakenly double booked two sets of couples. The guests arrived at the hotel at midday ready to check in for the weekend. I commenced the checking-in procedure and it was then that I realised the rooms had already been taken. In addition to this problem, we were fully booked and had no spare rooms to offer them as an alternative. I decided that the best way to approach the problem was to be honest with them and tell them about the mistake that we had made. However, I felt that the best place to break the news was in a quiet room away from the reception area. I asked my colleague to take over the reception desk and I asked the guests to follow me to a conference room, which was out of the way.

I sat them down and began to explain what had happened in a calm and apologetic manner. Naturally, they were annoyed and disappointed with the situation. I reassured them that we would do everything in our power to resolve the issue. I then informed them that I would need a short amount of time to resolve the issue and asked them to remain in the bar area where they would be served complimentary drinks and food.

I then went away to speak to the duty manager and to request permission to seek alternative accommodation which the hotel would pay for. I returned to the group and explained that the hotel would try to arrange other accommodation in the area, to an equal or higher standard than that which they had booked with us. I explained that we would refund their payment in full as well as paying for the new hotel room, as compensation for the inconvenience caused. They agreed to this and appeared to be happy with the level of service I was offering them.

The situation was eventually resolved after I had managed to find alternative accommodation for the guests in the local area. The following week, I followed up with a letter to both couples, further apologising and offering them a discounted rate for any future visits. Since then, one of the couples has returned to the hotel and used our services."

"Please supply any additional information which you feel might benefit your application."

This type of question serves one purpose – the opportunity for you to sell yourself. The type of response you provide will be very much dependant on your own experiences, personality and attributes. If you are given the opportunity to supply additional information, then you should do. Within your response, summarise your skills, experience and attributes whilst reiterating the reasons why you want to join their team. Always make sure you end on a positive note!

Finally, before submitting your application, make sure you read each response and check for mistakes, grammar and punctuation. Remember that you are trying to create a professional image on paper. First impressions are important, even if they are paper-based!

Response Example:

"I have been working hard to research both the role that I am applying for and the tour operator I have chosen to join. I have taken my application seriously and have studied the qualities and attributes that are required of a competent holiday rep and I believe I would be a valuable asset to your team.

My experience and skills already gained in my working life will stand me in good stead to become a professional, reliable and dedicated employee.

Thank you for taking the time to read my application."

CHAPTER FOUR

THE ASSESSMENT DAY

INTRODUCTION

For the majority of tour operators, the assessment day will consist of the following:

- Introduction

- Written tests (including the maths & brochure test)

- Team assessments & role plays

- Final Interview

The assessment day normally comes after the application form stage so if you have progressed this far, well done! Remember, it is not always the loudest and most talkative people that pass the interview stages. Interviewers are also looking for calm, friendly and imaginative people to join their company.

KEY POINT TO REMEMBER: As soon as you arrive the recruitment team are watching you and taking notes; you may not even be aware this is happening. Therefore, as soon as you arrive (even while you are waiting for the day to begin) you must start talking and interacting with other candidates. Do not just sit there in the corner by yourself while the other candidates talk to each other. This creates a bad impression and you need to show that communication and teamwork are key skills you possess.

CREATING A GOOD IMPRESSION

You only get one chance to create a first impression, so use it wisely. In fact, many people form a first impression within the first seven seconds of meeting someone. Research shows that 96% of the impact of a first impression is formed on non-verbal communication, i.e. how we speak and how we look and behave. So, as you stand in front of the recruitment staff you need to ensure you are giving the right signals.

When you attend the assessment centre we advise that you wear a coordinating suit (ladies – jacket and skirt, gentlemen – jacket and trousers).

Although it is purely down to individual preference, we recommend your shoes are flat soled or flat heeled. The essential part in relation to your shoes is to make sure that you have polished them thoroughly. Ensure your nails are clean and that your hair is tidy – getting it cut the day before would not be a bad thing. Also, make sure that you come across in a confident manner, but do not be overconfident – there is a fine line. Nobody likes an arrogant person, so make sure you are not over the top in terms of your confidence.

Your body language plays an important part throughout

the selection process, so make sure you are aware of your posture. When sitting down, sit upright. When standing, stand tall and do not slouch. Be proud of yourself and who you are and above all – smile and enjoy yourself!

FACIAL EXPRESSION AND EYE CONTACT

Make sure that you are smiling and that you exude warmth and friendliness. Of course, it is unrealistic to expect you to smile all of the time but it will help you to relax and it is an aspect of your personality that the recruitment staff will be looking for on the day. It is a good idea to ask your friends and family what they think of your body language and how you come across to them. Try to ask someone who will give you an honest answer and not just something that you want to hear. Eye contact is essential and if you are a shy person then you will need to work on this.

Eye contact shows that you are confident in nature, which forms part of the qualities and attributes that we discussed in a previous section. However, there is a fine line between making eye contact and staring at a person. Continually staring at somebody in the eyes can be confrontational and off-putting. Try looking around the eyes at different points in a triangular formation just to break up the eye contact.

COMMUNICATION

Communication is not just about having the ability to talk to people. It also involves listening too. There are basically two different forms of listening skills – verbal and non-verbal.

Verbal listening skills utilise the spoken word to agree, confirm or explore, whilst somebody is talking. Simple words and

phrases such as 'yes, I agree', 'that must have been awful'; 'I can see your point of view' are all used to let a person know that we are listening to what they are saying.

Non-verbal listening skills are purely facial expressions, which again let somebody know that you are listening to them. For example, a simple nod of the head informs a person that you understand or agree with what they are saying. Also frowning, smiling and laughing are all forms of non-verbal communication skills.

Throughout the assessment, you will need to demonstrate effective communication skills, both verbal and non-verbal. We recommend that you practice these skills prior to attending the assessment and make sure that you are not false but sincere, in all of your actions.

BE ENTHUSIASTIC

There is no doubt that enthusiasm can win people over. An enthusiastic person can bring great benefits to a team and you will want to demonstrate that you are enthusiastic about the tour operator you are applying to join. If you are there just going through the motions then the recruitment staff will pick up on this. Be the enthusiastic person amongst the crowd and get involved whenever the opportunity arises. If a volunteer is asked for, then put your hand up. You have come a long way and prepared hard for the assessment. Do everything you can to improve your chances on the day.

BE CONFIDENT, BUT NOT OVER-CONFIDENT!

Confidence is an important asset of the holiday rep. You will have to deal with situations on a daily basis that require

your strength of character, assertiveness and confidence. However, there is a fine line between confidence and over-confidence. Throughout the selection process, demonstrate your confidence, but do not overdo it.

Over-confidence is arrogance and it is not wanted in the tour operator industry.

PUNCTUALITY

The tour operator industry wants to provide a service that is on time, every time, and it therefore requires its staff to be the same. Make sure that you are not late for any part of the selection process. Plan your journey to the assessment centre well in advance, and if you are worried about the traffic, then it might be a good idea to invest in hotel accommodation close to the venue the night before.

Problems such as not knowing where to park, road works or getting lost are all common experiences that the ill-prepared candidate will encounter. Be prepared and cover every eventuality. The last thing you want to happen is to get off on the wrong foot by being late. If you live close by, or are within driving distance, then try a dry run the day before your assessment. Drive to the assessment centre the day before, find out exactly where it is and time your journey so you can prepare yourself for the actually journey. It would be better to get lost on your dry run the day before than on the actual day of your assessment and get yourself all hot and flustered.

WHAT TO WEAR FOR YOUR INTERVIEW AND IS 'SAFE' GOOD?

Many people dress to feel safe at the interview. Whilst this

is not a problem, why not try being a little bolder in your choice of colours? Have a look at the colour scheme of the holiday rep uniform for the tour operator you are applying to join. When choosing your outfit and its colour, take into consideration the tour operator's image.

MALES – SHOES

Make sure that you shoes are clean and well-polished. Having dirty or untidy shoes says a lot about you as a person. If you are not used to cleaning your shoes, then now is a good time to begin. Use real shoe polish and a brush and don't just go over them with a silicone cleaner.

CLEANLINESS

Your personal cleanliness is very important. Your hair should be washed and well-styled, unless you don't have any, of course. It is advised that you avoid any wild colours or styles and if your hair is coloured, make sure that no roots are showing. Hands and nails should also be clean and not bitten.

YOUR SUIT

It is a good idea to invest in a quality suit, if you can afford it. Choose a quality material and not one that is likely to crease easily. If you are driving to the interview then make sure you take off your jacket before setting out, as it can easily become creased at the back whilst sitting down.

YOUR TIE

Choose a tie that reflects your personality. It should be of a formal nature and not stand out for the wrong reasons. Once again, consider the image of the tour operator and the colour scheme they use.

FACIAL HAIR

Unfortunately, most tour operators will not accept facial hair so we advise that you turn up clean shaven. It is worthwhile checking with the tour operator first about their policy in relation to facial hair.

FEMALES – PERSONAL CLEANLINESS

This is vital; as we are sure you are aware. Try to think of any holidays you have been on in the past. What do you remember about the holiday rep? Were they well presented? The image that the tour operator wants to portray is of vital importance and your image should reflect that image. Your hands and nails are continually on show whilst working as a holiday rep member and therefore they need to be clean, well-manicured and looked after. Your choice of nail varnish is your own, but we recommend that you do wear some.

SHOES

Make sure that your shoes are well cleaned and polished with no scuffs or scrapes. We recommend that you wear court shoes for the selection process, although this is not vital.

YOUR CHOICE OF HAIRSTYLE

The most important thing in relation to your choice of hairstyle is that you feel confident with how you look. You can wear your hair up or down, the choice is yours, but if you do decide to wear your hair up, then make sure there are no strands or bits sticking out anywhere. Make sure it is washed and styled and looking good. Your hair says a lot about who you are, so that extra time spent on it, will go a long way.

WEAR A PROFESSIONAL-LOOKING SUIT

It is important, once again, to make sure that you feel good and comfortable with whatever you choose to wear. A skirt, dress or suit are all acceptable and the choice of colour is totally down to you. We mentioned earlier that some colours are safe and whilst there is no problem with a safe colour, you might impress with something that is a little bit more daring and you will be guaranteed to stand out from the majority of people who will be wearing grey, blue or black.

The best advice is to try a few outfits on and see what you think looks best. Make sure that whatever you decide to wear is comfortable, doesn't crease easily and is of good quality. Remember to consider matching the colours that represent the tour operator.

HOW TO LOOK YOUR BEST

Making sure you get enough sleep is vital to keeping your energy levels up, and eating a well-balanced diet will go a long way to keeping you focused and determined prior to and during the holiday rep selection process.

The saying 'we are what we eat' is very true and a diet of regular alcohol, fast food and cigarettes is not the most effective way to maintaining a healthy look. Of course, we all need to relax and enjoy ourselves, but being disciplined and making sure you get sufficient sleep before the assessment day is essential.

YOUR ASSESSMENT DAY INTRODUCTION

At the beginning of the day the tour operator recruitment staff will ask each candidate to introduce themselves to them and the other members of the group. This is the first chance they will get to see you and what you are about. It is your first opportunity to create a positive impact, so you need to ensure you prepare your introduction in advance, and rehearse it.

Many candidates will not prepare an introduction or will not be ready for it, so having one prepared beforehand is a good thing. The areas that you should try to cover during your introduction are as follows: Your name, where you live, your current or previous occupation, interests, hobbies and ambitions, and what you have achieved.

YOUR INTRODUCTION

Take a look at the following introduction and see how effective it is:

"Good morning everybody, it's a pleasure to be here and meet you all! My name is Lucy and I'm 23 years old. My current job is as a waitress for a local Italian restaurant which I absolutely love. I get great satisfaction from helping our guests and making their stay the more enjoyable. The tips are also quite good too!

At the moment I am living in Woking, but if I am successful in my ambition to become a holiday rep with this tour operator, I will be relocating to xxxx.

Recently, I raised £500 for a local charity by taking part in a tandem skydive. The skydive was from 12,000 feet and by the time I reached that height I was starting to wonder if I had made the right decision! I am so happy to be here today, and to have been given the opportunity of fulfilling a life-long dream of becoming holiday rep. I can't wait to meet you all and look forward to talking to so many great people, thanks."

The introduction is positive and, therefore, should be portrayed in this manner. She talks about a charity event where she raised money for a good cause. She also uses a small amount of humour which works very well. She talks about her current role which is customer-focused and that he enjoys it very much. Remember, never to put down or criticise your employer. This is not a good thing to do and it will be frowned upon. When it is your turn to stand up and introduce yourself, stand tall, be positive, enthusiastic and cheerful. Be genuinely glad to be at the assessment day and look forward to the whole process.

A good tip to help you stand out from all your other classmates is to stand up when you give your introduction. The majority of candidates will remain seated as they will be nervous about introducing themselves in front of people they have only just met. However, by standing up and introducing yourself you are saying to the assessors that you are a confident person (even though you maybe nervous as well) and this is a key skill they will be looking for. Using a blank sheet of paper, create your own introduction, based on your own personal circumstances.

THE ASSESSMENT DAY WRITTEN TESTS

The majority of tour operators will ask you to sit a short mathematics test and a brochure test. The pass mark and number of questions will vary from tour operator to tour operator but it is approximately 70%.

Once you have passed the application process and have been invited to take part in the assessment day the tour operator will confirm with you what you need to prepare and which tests you are required to sit. Instead of a brochure test some operators may ask you to sit a simple English test. You are given a set of sentences and you have to correct the grammar and the spelling.

The mathematics test includes basic forms of addition, subtraction, multiplication and division. The brochure test is a general knowledge test based on the information which is contained within their brochure/s. Many candidates fail to prepare for this part of the assessment day and are surprised when they do not reach the pass mark to progress to the next stage.

MATHEMATICS TEST

The most effective way to prepare for the mathematics test is to practice basic currency and percentage questions. As a holiday rep, you will be required to perform basic mathematical sums when booking excursions and when dealing with customers change.

On the following page we have provided you with a mathematics test to help you prepare. Write down your answers on a blank sheet of paper or use the answer sheet provided on the following page. Tip – Make Sure you take a

calculator with you on the day! Many candidates forget to take one with them. Using a calculator is essential to making the best use of your time and increases your chances of reaching the correct answer.

GOOD LUCK.

MATHEMATICAL CALCULATION TEST

This type of test is designed to test your basic arithmetic skills.

It will test your ability in relation to addition, subtraction, multiplication and division and is an ideal way of practising for psychometric tests. By practising these tests, you will find that your ability to work quickly and accurately under pressure will improve.

The use of a calculator is not permitted during these tests and you should not use one when attempting the following exercise. In each question a mathematical sum is given with one area missing. This missing area is the one you must identify as the answer.

For example:

$5 + 10 = 15 - ?$

Answer = 1, 0, 2, 4, 3

The answer to this question is 0.

Explanation: $5 + 10 = 15$, so therefore $15 - 0 = 15$.

MATHEMATICAL CALCULATION TEST

EXERCISE 1

1. $37 + ? = 95$

2. $86 - ? - 32$

3. $? - 104 = 210$

4. $109 \times ? = 218$

5. $6 + 9 + 15 = 15 \times ?$

6. $34 + 13 - 4 = ? + 3$

7. 35 divide $? = 10 + 7.5$

8. $7 \times ? = 28 \times 3$

9. 100 divide $4 = 67 - ?$

10. $32 \times 9 = 864$ divide ?

11. $11 \times ? = 265 - 144$

12. $14 \times 28 = ?$

13. $(4000 + 56)$ divide $? = 1014$

14. $(32 \times 2) \times 4 = 512 - ?$

15. $2.5 \times 3 = 37.5$ divide ?

16. (8 divide by 2) $\times 16 = 150 - ?$

17. $87 - 1 = (45 - 2) \times ?$

18. $(17 + 15) - 8 = ? \times 3$

19. $(7 \times 10) \times 3 = ? \times 6$

20. $(19 + 19)$ divide $19 = (? \times 2)$ divide 2

ANSWERS TO EXERCISE 1

1. 58

    The quickest way to get to the answer is to subtract 37 from 95 which leaves 58.

2. 54

    Subtract 32 from 86 to be left with 54.

3. 314

    Add 210 to 104 to get 314.

4. 2

    Divide 218 by 109 to get the answer of 2.

5. 2

    6 + 9 + 15 = 30 so therefore 15 multiplied by 2 gives you 30.

6. 40

    34 + 13 = 47. Then subtract 4 to be left with 43. Therefore 40+3 gives you 43.

7. 2

    10+7.5 will give you 17.5; therefore 15 divided by 2 will give you 17.5.

8. 12

    28 × 3 will give you 84; therefore 7 × 12 will also give you 84.

9. 42

    100 divided by 4 will give you 25; therefore 67-25 will leave you with 42.

10. 3

    32 × 9 will give you 288. Now multiply 288 by 3 to get 864.

11. 11

   265-164 gives you 121; therefore 11 multiplied by 11 will also give you 121.

12. 392

   14 × 28 will give you 392.

13. 4

   (4000 + 56) gives you 4056. Divide 4056 by the answer 1014 to get the answer 4.

14. 256

   32 × 2 will give you 64. Then multiply 64 by 4 to get 256. 512 – 256 leaves you with 256.

15. 5

   2.5 × 3 will give you 7.5, then 37.5 divided by 5 will leave you with 7.5

16. 86

   8 divided by 2 will give you 4. Then multiply 4 by 16 to get 64. Then 150 subtract 86 will leave you with 64.

17. 2

   87 – 1 will give you 86. Then, 45 – 2 will give you 43. Multiply 43 by 2 to reach 86.

18. 8

   17+15 will give you 32. Subtract 8 from 32 to be left with 24. Then multiply 8 by 3 to be left with the same figure 24.

19. 35

   7 × 10 will give you 70 which when multiplied by 3 will give you 210. Then 35 × 6 equals the same figure 210.

20. 2

   19 + 19 will give you 38 which, when divided by 19, will give you 2. Then 2 × 2 will give you 4 which, when divided by 2, will give you the answer 2.

Below are 5 examples of the types of currency and percentage questions that you will be asked to work out during your assessment day. As with every other stage of the assessment process you need to show that you are an able candidate. The questions have been written in a step by step format so that you see exactly how the answer was achieved.

Q1. You sell theme park tickets for €50 each and earn 5% on each tick you sell, how much do you earn in GBP and Euros.

Answer:

50 (Euros) = 100% and you need to work out what 5% equals

The easiest way to do this is first work out what 1% equals. And to do this you divide you 50 Euros by 100:

50 ÷ 100 = 0.5 (What this means is that 1% equals 0.5 Euros)

Therefore, to work out 5% you multiply 0.5 by 5:

0.5 × 5 = 2.5 Euros

So, for every ticket you sell you earn 2.5 Euros

Q2. If £1 = €1.40 and you sell €1,600 of trips at your welcome meeting, how much is that in £GBP?

Answer:

Remember, for every £1 you get €1.40 Euros so when converting your €1,600 back into pounds the amount in pounds has to be smaller.

So, to work out the pounds you take the amount of Euros made (which in this case is 1600) and divide by €1.40 (which is what one pound equals).

€1,600 ÷ €1.40 = £1142.86

So from the sales meeting you have made £1142.86 in sales

Q3. You are told that the current exchange rate is: £1 = €1.40

a) 3 × €42 = €126. How much is that in pounds?

b) How much is £54 in Euros?

This is similar to the question above where you have to convert Euros into pounds and then pounds into Euros. You just apply the same method as the question above.

Answer:

a) So in total you have €126 and 1 pound is equal to €1.40. To work out the number of pounds you divide your total by the exchange rate (which in this case is 1.40).

€126 ÷ €1.40 = £90

So the total in pounds is £90.

b) This is just a reverse of question a) and instead of starting with Euros and working out the amount in pounds you are starting with pounds and converting to Euros.

So, how much is £54 in Euros?

If £1 = 1.40 Euros then £54 = (54 × 1.40) = €75.60

Q4. Work out the percentage of people from the new arrivals that attended your welcome meeting.

You go to the airport and you pick up a total 130 new arrivals and you inform them that at 8 o'clock in morning you will be holding a welcome meeting. In the morning 50 of the new arrivals attend welcome meeting. What is the % turnout?

This question is straight forward when using your calculator.

Remember in the above questions you are dealing with currency and now you are being asked to workout the percentage of people that turned up to your meeting. The answer that you arrive at should never be more than 100%. If you do arrive at an answer greater than this recheck your calculation.

Answer:

If 50 people out of 130 attend then to calculate the percentage you divide 50 by 130 and the multiply by 100:

$50 \div 130 = 0.38461538$, then multiply this by 100 to work out the percentage.

$0.38461538 \times 100 = 38.46\%$

Therefore, 38.46% (which realistically means 38%) of the new arrivals attended the welcome meeting.

Q5. Here's another currency question and answer to work through:

You have picked up your first lot of customers from the airport and are on the shuttle bus back to the hotel. You have counted the amount of new arrivals and there are 36. You tell them that you are having a welcome meeting tomorrow morning at 10am and it would be great to see them all there. You arrive in the morning to find that 28 out of the 36 new arrivals have turned up for your meeting. Calculate the turnout?

Before we go through the answer take spend a couple of minutes working out the answer for yourself.

Answer:

$28 \div 36 = 0.7777 \times 100 = 77.77\%$ (which if you round up to the nearest % gives you 78%).

BROCHURE TEST

Some tour operators will ask you to sit a brochure general knowledge test as part of their selection process. The pass mark can vary but it is usually between the 70% -80% mark and there are usually only 5 questions in this test.

Once your application has been successful your tour operator will inform you to see whether they will require you to sit this type of test. If you have not received any information from your tour operator about your assessment day make sure you contact them in advance to find out what is required of you. The key to passing the assessment day is preparation and if you don't know what they want you to prepare you will struggle on the day!

The key is to read through the brochures that the company informs you there will be a test on. Although there are only typically 5 questions on this part of the assessment you should not leave this to the last minute The type and nature of the questions that you will be asked during this test vary, however the general type of questions will be centred around what's new for this year, current destinations, what they offer their customers and their special offers.

Examples of Questions:

1. What are the children's clubs called?
2. Where are the holiday villages?
3. What is the airline called?
4. What are the top destinations that we fly to in Europe?
5. What long haul destinations do we fly to?
6. Are there any new destinations this year?
7. What special offers do we have this year?

8. What is the new product in Spain?

9. What does the gold member caters for?

10. When was the company established?

It is also vital to your success that you pay attention to what you are told throughout the assessment day. When you first arrive you will be given a brief introduction about the company, the role of a holiday rep and your development as a holiday rep. Listen very carefully to what you are told about the company as this can come up as a question later on!

Some tour operators will also ask you to sit a simple English test. The idea here is that you read through a paragraph or a number of sentences and you have to correct any mistakes in terms of grammar or spelling.

PRESENTATION

The majority of tour operators will ask you to prepare a 2-3 minute presentation for you to deliver to the rest of the group at some point during the assessment day. The presentation maybe based on a favourite destination or you may be required to try and to sell something to the panel, like a beach party. If you have not been asked to prepare a presentation then do not panic. This may form part of your assessment day where you are actually given time on the day to put together a presentation. By reading through this section you will gain and understanding of the types of hot topics you may be asked to present on.

The presentation is another opportunity for you to show the recruitment staff that you possess the qualities they are looking for. You need to show that you are confident standing up in front of a group of people and that you can

communicate in an effective manner. This will be vital for your role as a holiday rep when holding welcome meetings and selling excursions.

As a result of this you must ensure that allow yourself enough time before the assessment day to prepare and practice your presentation. By putting time and effort into developing your presentation you will demonstrate to the recruitment staff your imagination and commitment to becoming a holiday rep.

Example's of Presentation topics:

- Prepare a 2 minute presentation on a holiday destination of your choice

- Prepare a 3 minute presentation on your favourite holiday

- Prepare a 2 minute presentation on a time when you gave/ received great customer service.

- Prepare a 2 minute presentation on where you would like to work as a holiday rep and why (think carefully about this one, it would be looked upon more favourably if you choose a destination that the tour operator actually files to).

- Prepare a presentation on where you see yourself in 10 years time

- Prepare a presentation on a product you could not live without and sell it to the rest of the group.

- Prepare a 2 minute presentation on yourself and present this back to the group.

- Prepare a 2 minute presentation based on an excursion you are selling at a welcome meeting.

These are just some examples of the types of presentations you may be asked to prepare before the assessment day. However, once you have applied you will have a greater understanding of what is required of you. For example, when preparing a presentation on a favourite holiday destination or the destination where you would like to work, remember there are a number of key factors to include. You may want to include the following:

- Where did you go?

- What was the weather like?

- What was there to see and do?

- Did you go on any excursions?

- What places did you eat at and what places would you recommend?

- Did you experience any good customer service?

- What was your rep like?

By mentioning all these things you are starting to present yourself in the same way as a holiday rep would if they were describing a local town.

The other type of topic you may be asked to present on is to sell something such as a boat trip or an object that you could not live with out.

This type of presentation is different to the presentation above as you are not only selling yourself but you also have to sell the object/product. This type of presentation is also likely to appear as a group exercise during the assessment day. The key point to remember when selling something is the feature and benefit rule.

Key to remember

The difference between a feature and a benefit is as follows:

A feature is something the product has or does, while a benefit is something it does for you.

- A **FEATURE** is one of the components or functions of your product.

- A **BENEFIT** is a way in which your product improves the life of the user.

To explain this in more clearly below you will find a worked example of how to apply the feature and benefit rule.

For example, if on the assessment day you were asked, on the spare of the moment, to present on an object you could not live with out, this may appear a daunting task. However, by simply applying the feature and benefit rule you can easily and calmly generate a sales pitch. In the example below the chosen object that you could not live without is a mobile phone. Once you have your chosen object you now need to put together a list of features.

Features

1.   Has a video recorder and camera

2.   Has a hard protective case

3.   Has internet access

4.   Has a removable battery

5.   Has a large expandable memory

6.   Has a FM radio

7.   Has a loud speaker

8.   Has an alarm

These are just some of the features that a particular mobile phone has. Once you have listed the features for your object you must now ask yourself what the benefit of that feature is to the customer. So now go back over the features and write next to them what the benefits are.

Benefits

1. To allow the person to take pictures/videos without having to carry a camera or video with them. It also allows them to easily share these pictures / videos with their friends.

2. This means that if the phone is accidently dropped on the floor it is protected.

3. Allows the user access the internet from their mobile phone without having to be on a computer or in an office. They also have access to the emails.

4. As the battery is easily accessible it can be changed if there any problems or if a new one is required by simply removing the back cover.

5. An expandable memory allows the user to insert a memory card into the phone which means they can now store a large number of their favourite songs on their phone. They can now listen to these when ever they chose.

6. This gives the user the option to listen to a number of different radio stations.

7. This allows the user to put the person they are speaking to one loud speaker and carrying doing other tasks at the same time. They could also use this function to listen to their music at a greater volume

8. An alarm is an essential function for the user to ensure that they wake up on time ensuring they are punctual to their holiday rep assessment day

The features and benefits of the mobile phone listed above are just a few that you could use and are just provided for the purpose of this example.

If you are performing a sales pitch on a particular excursion then start by picking a feature of the day/place/excursion and explain clearly what the feature is and how that will benefit the person going. Then move onto the next feature and benefit. Keeping going until you have a list of features and benefits and this will now form the core of your presentation. Now that you understand the feature and benefit rule you can apply this on the day.

TIPS FOR PREPARING YOUR PRESENTATION

Your presentation provides an important opportunity for you to tell your audience about your chosen topic. The tips outlined below are intended to help you in planning your presentation.

The key to a good presentation is preparation. Try to get a relative or a friend to listen to your presentation and ask them to provide feedback. Try to practice the presentation more than once. The more times your practice the more confident you will become about delivering it on the day. We know that this may be difficult, as some tour operators do not ask you to prepare a presentation and tell you that time will be given to prepare on the day. Even if this is this case you can still begin to think of the topics that might come up and write down what you would include in them.

- Be the first person to put their hand up when asked who wants to give their presentation first. There are two reasons for this. Firstly, it shows that you are confident, motivated and organised, which will create a great impression. Secondly, as you are the first person to go you do not have the pressure of going after someone who has just delivered a really great presentation.

- When you first start your presentation focus on a friendly face as this will help calm any nerves and build your confidence

- Know, understand and organise all of your material on your chosen topic in a way that allows you to present it to the group.

- Practice and rehearse your speech more than once. The more times you practice, the more confident you will become and the better you will perform on the day.

- Record yourself delivering your presentation and then listen to yourself as you replay the recording. Did you sound confident? Did you talk too fast or mumble? You can use this as a way of improving your presentation.

- Try to look confident, calm and appear relaxed, even if you feel nervous. Your presentations are a chance for the management teams to see your ability to tell a story, stay focused and remember you are selling yourself.

- Speak slowly and clearly and with enthusiasm so that everyone in the room can hear and believe what you are saying. In addition, use eye contact to make everyone in your audience feel they are part of the presentation (this includes the examiner).

- Don't be afraid to pause during your presentation. A pause can have a powerful effect of keeping your

audience interested and intrigued about what you have to say. This will also ensure that you do not rush through your presentation.

- Try to project positive body language. Standing tall, keeping your head up, Smiling, walking or moving about is much more positive than sitting down or standing still with head down and reading from a sheet of paper.

- **SMILE.** This is not only important for your presentation but critical to the entire assessment day. Candidates have been unsuccessful because they did not smile enough! Even if your presentation goes wrong, keeping going and keep smiling.

- Use visual aids or props to enhance your presentation and make it stand out from every other presentation. By making your presentation unique and different it will create a positive image in the eyes of the recruitment staff. They are also more likely to remember a presentation that is unique.

- Try not to read straight from your notes. Although you may be nervous, this has a negative effect as it shows you are not confident and this is one of the attributes the recruitment team are looking for. There is no problem if you glance at your notes (or cards) for reference and if you make an error just simply correct it and carry on with your presentation.

- Try and add humour whenever appropriate and possible. This will lighten the mood and make you and everyone else feel at ease.

- When using PowerPoint for your presentation, be sure all necessary equipment is available. Always make sure

that you have a backup in place. For example, make sure you have handouts that you can give out which contains all the main points.

- Try to end your presentation, summarise your main points and try to finish your presentation with an interesting remark.

If you are using PowerPoint to deliver you presentation:

1. Keep information on any given slide to a minimum.

2. Too much information can make it difficult to read.

3. If you decide to use graphics, they need to be large enough to be easily read by the group.

4. Try not to over-complicate your presentation with too many graphics.

5. Use a font size that makes it easy to read.

6. When creating your slides, select a template that is easy on the eye, but not distracting.

7. Use a large font to highlight important ideas

8. Try not to fill your slides with information and simply read your presentation off each slide. Put then main points up and the expand on each point

9. Always make sure you have a back up in case the computer fails or is not available on the day.

10. Try to deliver your speech directly to your audience with occasional glances at the slides.

ROLE PLAYS

As part of your assessment you will have to perform a role play and this is usually on a one-to-one basis with one of the interviewers. Your role will be that of the holiday rep who has to deal with a customer who has a particular problem. The role of the customer, often an angry customer, is played by one of the recruitment staff. The idea is that you have to listen to their problem then come up with a solution.

TIP – Make sure you are prepared and aware that the interviewer will try and make this as realistic as possible. Do not be surprised if they start shouting and screaming at you!

The content of the role play will change. It will depend on you, your performance throughout the day and the company. Other companies might well ask you to do it as part of a group. The team are looking for you to be calm, perform under pressure and deal with it. The recruitment staff are not looking so much for the solution that you provide the customer, but the way you go about dealing with the complaint.

There are a number of vital stages to correctly dealing and handling a complaint and it is critical to your success that you know what these are. In the section below you will find the correct way to deal with a complaint, and if you can demonstrate an understanding of this in your role play, it will increase your chances of success.

When preparing for role plays try and think of the different types of complaints that a holiday rep would receive. Or even try to think of a complaint you have made yourself when you were on holiday.

Examples of role play situations:

- You have to deal with a complaint from an angry couple. They are unhappy with an excursion you had sold them during the welcome meeting.

- A young woman has come to you complaining that the air conditioning in her room does not work.

- A customer has come to you to complain that their luggage has gone missing at the airport and they are very unhappy.

- An elderly gentlemen is complaining that he paid for a room with a sea view and instead he has a room overlooking the car park.

- A customer has been told by the hotel reception staff that his room was double booked and apparently the hotel is now fully booked.

After reading the section below take a blank piece of paper and write down exactly how you would deal with these role play situations.

HOW TO DEAL WITH COMPLAINTS

Within the role play you will play the position of a holiday rep that has to deal with a particular customer and help to solve their problem. The information below reveals how to correctly deal with a customer complaint and if you can apply this during your role play, you will score highly with the examiners.

Try to imagine yourself as customer at a holiday resort. The service has not been fantastic and you want to complain. Are you concerned about the fact that one of the holiday rep staff went sick at the last minute and the team are short? No, of

course you're not. In fact, all you are concerned with is that your complaint gets dealt with quickly and effectively. During your career as a holiday rep, you will be faced with highly stressful situations in relation to difficult customers and you will need to react appropriately.

In any industry or profession where a customer is complaining, there are a number of key areas that the complainant is concerned with:

- They want someone to listen to their complaint.

- They want someone to understand why they are complaining.

- They want someone to sort out their complaint as soon as possible.

- They would like an apology.

- They want someone to explain what has gone wrong.

Holiday reps are required to deal with complaints in an efficient and effective manner. If you are successful in your application, your training course will cover these core skills in detail. However, having the knowledge of how to deal with customer complaints during the selection process will assist you. You may be asked a question, during the interview, that relates to customer complaints and having the ability to explain how they are dealt with is a positive aspect.

When dealing with customer complaints in any form, you will need to follow an action plan. This action plan is explained in detail on the following pages. The plan follows a structured format and each area follows on systematically from the other.

To begin with, you will listen to the complaint using effective verbal and non-verbal listening skills. The majority of people

associate communication skills primarily with the spoken word. However, these cover a number of areas. Having the ability to actively listen is a key factor to resolving the complaint successfully. Take a look at the stages of dealing with complaints before reading each individual section.

At the end of the explanations we have provided you with a 'Dealing with Complaints' exercise to help you put these skills into practice.

- Listen to the complaint.

- Apologise and appreciate.

- Gather information.

- Provide a solution.

- Reach an agreement.

- Take action.

- Follow up.

LISTEN TO THE COMPLAINT

One of the most important factors, when dealing with the complaint, is to listen. Listening effectively can be done in a number of ways. This can be achieved through facial expression, body language, oral confirmation and clarification techniques. If the customer is sat down then you may wish to crouch down to their level. This will alleviate any confrontational body position where you are looking down at the complainant. This will also prevent the need for speaking any louder than necessary. Then, listen to the complaint in full.

Maintain good eye contact throughout, nod, use an interested facial expression and confirm back to the passenger what they have told you. If the passenger begins to shout, becomes aggressive or confrontational, or even starts swearing, then you will have to be assertive in your response and inform them that their language will not be tolerated. Inform them that you want to deal with their complaint quickly and to their satisfaction, but it must be done in a calm manner.

APOLOGISE AND APPRECIATE

Once you have listened to their complaint, you need to apologise and explain that you fully understand how they feel. This will usually have the effect of defusing any confrontation and will make the complainant feel that they are being heard. It is all about establishing a rapport with the passenger and making them feel that their complaint is important.

The following is a sample response to a customer's complaint:

"Thank you for taking the time, sir, to explain what the problem is. If the same situation had happened to me I would certainly feel as you do."

In just two sentences, you have made the complainant feel valued and understood. Now you can begin to resolve the issue and you will find it easier to talk to them from now on.

Providing their complaint is genuine, you should now take ownership of the complaint and see it through to a successful resolution. You have listened to their complaint and acknowledged there is an issue. Now move on to establishing the facts, which will give you the tools to create a successful resolution.

GATHER INFORMATION

When dealing with a complaint as a holiday rep, the next important stage is to gather as much essential information as possible. The reason for doing this is that it will allow you to make a more informed judgement about the situation and it will also allow you to take steps to prevent it from happening again.

Complaints take time to deal with and detract you from other important duties. When a member of the team is dealing with a complaint, the rest of team must make up for the deficit in numbers. Therefore, if the situation that led to the complaint in the first instance can be avoided in the future, this will allow the holiday rep staff to concentrate on their primary role – providing a high level of customer service to all customers.

When gathering information, concentrate on the following areas:

- What is the complaint in relation to?
- What are the facts of the incident?
- Who was responsible?
- How would the passenger like the problem to be resolved?

Once you have gathered all of the facts, you will then be able to take action to resolve the issue.

PROVIDE A SOLUTION

Coming up with a suitable solution to the customer's complaint can be difficult, especially if they are reluctant to accept any reasonable offering. Therefore, it is important that you remain calm throughout.

Make sure that the solution/s you offer are relevant to the situation and are achievable. If they are not, then do not make the mistake of offering something you cannot deliver. This will just make the situation worse. When providing a solution, ask the customer if your offer is acceptable. For example:

"Would you like me to arrange another room for you?" or
"Would you like me to see if we have an alternative hotel?"

By offering different solutions to the complainant you are asking them to make the decision for you, and therefore making your life easier. This way, they will end up getting what they want and, therefore, will be happy with the resolution.

Remember – when dealing with the complaint, never take it personally and never be rude or confrontational.

REACH AN AGREEMENT

Once you have offered the solution, make sure you get the complainants approval first. This will prevent them from complaining about the action you are taking to resolve the issue. The most effective method of achieving this is through verbal acknowledgement.

For example:

"Ok, sir, to resolve the issue, I will go away and organise another room for you. I will make sure, this time, that the room has a sea view. Is this alright with you?"

Reaching an agreement is important psychologically. The passenger will feel that you are being considerate to their needs and by reaffirming the solution with them you are showing them that you have their interests at heart.

TAKE ACTION

Now that you have reached an agreement, get on with the task in hand. If it is going to take you a while to take the action agreed upon, you might find it useful to inform the customer.

"Ok, I will now go and sort out your new room. This might take me a few minutes, so please bear with me."

CHAPTER FIVE

TEAM ASSESSMENTS

GROUP EXERCISES

Group exercises form another integral part of the holiday rep selection process. The tour operator recruitment staff will be looking for candidates to demonstrate specific qualities throughout the team assessment.

Many employers use group exercises to test a candidate's performance and ability, and they are a very good indicator of someone's confidence, motivation and enthusiasm. The team assessment stage will usually require you, and a number of other potential candidates, to come up with a solution to a problem, all within a specific time frame. During the exercise, you will be given a scenario to deal with and you'll have to decide amongst yourselves the most appropriate method of resolving the issue.

During the exercise, you will often see candidates fighting to get their views across. Many candidates will start talking over the top of other people, but this is not the best way to approach the assessment. This is where you will have the opportunity to demonstrate you have the right qualities to work as part of a team and come up with answers to problems.

The solution or answer that the team come up with doesn't have to be the right one. However, the panel are looking for you come up with a logical solution.

AN EXPLANATION

The number of candidates taking part in the team assessment will vary from tour operator to tour operator, but to give you an idea, there are usually about a dozen.

At the beginning of the group exercise you will be provided with a brief and you will then be given a set time in order to come up with a solution. Throughout the team assessment you will have a member of the tour operator recruitment staff monitoring the session and scoring each of you individually. The important thing to remember, during the group exercise, is how you present yourself. Yes, it is good to provide a solution to the problem, but there is so much more to the assessment than problem solving. Here are the key areas that you will be assessed on during the assessment.

Take a look at each assessable area before moving onto the sample exercises.

HOW TO SCORE POSITIVELY

AREA NUMBER 1 – INVOLVING OTHERS

During the assessment, you must try to involve other people. If during the assessment, you notice a person who is not getting involved or saying anything, try to involve them. Ask them a question such as – "What do you think we should do?" You will receive positive marks for involving others during the assessment.

AREA NUMBER 2 – COMMUNICATION SKILLS

Use effective listening skills throughout the assessment, both verbal and non-verbal. Make sure you listen to what other people are saying and use facial expressions and actions to indicate that you are doing so.

AREA NUMBER 3 – POSITIVE TEAMWORKING

During the assessment, make an effort to get on with the group. Smile, be positive and show that you have the ability to work effectively in a team environment. Don't try to show off or gain points by doing things on your own. Yes, come up with positive solutions, but involve the group and get involved with them.

AREA NUMBER 4 – MAKING POSITIVE CONTRIBUTIONS

Try to think of positive solutions to the problem. Remember that you don't have to necessarily solve the problem totally, but do try to come up with a logical solution and one that would work. If somebody doesn't agree with your solution, be willing to change or accept that maybe there is a better idea.

AREA 5 – PROVIDE POSITIVE FEEDBACK

If somebody comes up with a good idea during the assessment, tell them so.

Provide encouragement to the group by saying phrases such as – "I think that's a great idea, which would work", or "Yes, I think that would work, because…"

AREA 6 – EFFECTIVE BODY LANGUAGE

Throughout the assessment, demonstrate positive body language. If you are sat down, do not slouch. Instead, sit upright and be enthusiastic about getting involved with the group. Be positive in your nature, smile and laugh where appropriate.

AREA 7 – BUILD ON IDEAS TO SOLVE THE PROBLEM

If a member of the group offers a solution, try to build on it. Don't dismiss people's ideas just because you don't agree with them. Look for ways to see if they will work.

SAMPLE GROUP EXERCISES

On the following page we have provided a sample team assessment exercise to help you prepare. Please note that tour operators use a variety of different scenarios and this is not the exact scenario that you will be presented with on the day. It is provided as a practice aid only. Remember that it is not the scenario that is important but, rather, how you deal with it effectively in the team environment. If you do not take part in the team assessments you are guaranteed to fail. Make sure you get involved!

SAMPLE GROUP EXERCISE 1

You have just been handed a letter of complaint by your manger from a guest that was at your resort only two weeks ago. For this exercise you have to read through the letter and discuss in your group the best way to deal with this complaint, how and what further action, if any, you should you take and how would to ensure that this does not happen again. You must then present your findings back to the group.

For this exercise, try to think about times when you have received great customer service, what it was that made it great and could you apply it to this situation? You should also consider how to satisfy the customer who has the complaint and also how you can learn from this to provide a better customer service in the future.

SAMPLE GROUP EXERCISE 2

Now that you have been split into groups, each group must now prepare a welcome meeting, discuss what you think is involved in a welcome meeting and then

present this welcome meeting to the rest of the group who will be acting as your customers who have just arrived. This exercise allows you to demonstrate to the recruitment staff that you can work as part of team and that confident at delivering a sales pitch. Make sure that everyone has something to say at the welcome meeting and that it is not dominated by one individual. For this exercise you could talk about the types of guests you are presenting to, are they young or old or mainly families? Would this affect your welcome meeting (if you have a young audience they are unlikely to be interested in the history of the country).

You may want to discuss how to make your pitch more entertaining through the use of visual aids such as pictures or when is the best time to have a welcome meeting. You also may want to discuss any warning that you should give to customer's e.g. sun block or poolside rules. Try to think of the welcome meetings you have been to and what was presented to you.

SAMPLE GROUP EXERCISE 3

For this exercise we are going to split you up into three groups and you must discuss the daily duties that you think a holiday rep performs. Once you have done this you will then present your findings back to the group.

For this exercise refer to the beginning of the guide which lists the responsibilities of a holiday rep.

You may also want to consider the type of paper work that a holiday rep would need to fill in and the sort of health and safety checks they would need to carry out.

SAMPLE GROUP EXERCISE 4

As part of the group exercise some holiday operators (especially the ones aimed at Club Reps) will ask you as part of your group exercise to prepare a dance / music routine and then perform it back to the group.

Even if you feel that singing or dancing are not your strongest qualities you must still ensure that you take part and perform well in a team!

ASSESMENT ADVICE

During the assessment, remember to focus on the relevant areas that you are trying to demonstrate. Don't become too concerned in providing a good solution to the problem or scenario. Keep your eye on the main objective.

If a member of the team is controlling the situation, talking too much and not allowing others to talk, tell them politely that you would like to talk. If you are not confident enough to do this, put your hand up.

Remember to involve others in the group. Don't get involved in an argument, even if somebody annoys you. Keep an eye on the time. You will only have a set amount of time to provide a solution.

Remember – you will score more points for involving others and providing positive feedback than you will for 'controlling' the team and talking over everybody. As hard as it may be, try to enjoy the assessment.

CHAPTER SIX

THE INTERVIEW

INTRODUCTION

The holiday rep selection panel are highly experienced in being able to determine who the right people for the job are. Therefore, it is vitally important that you prepare well for this next stage. If you have been successful in passing the preceding stages then congratulations. You now need some guidance and advice on how to prepare for, and pass, the interview stage of the process.

The first stage of your preparation is research. Research, in terms of the role you are applying for and the particular tour operator you are hoping to join, is essential. During the interview, you are likely to be asked questions relating to the following areas:

- What you know about the role of a holiday rep.

- The reasons for applying and why you want to join this particular tour operator.

- What you know about the tour operator.

- How you deal with specific situations in your working life and what you learn from them.

- Challenges faced by the tour operator.

- Your own personal qualities and attributes.

- Your strengths and weaknesses.

- Team-working skills

- Respect and diversity

Before we go on to look at the questions you are likely to face during your interview, let's take a look at some other important factors about the interview.

FIRST IMPRESSIONS

Remember – you only get one chance to make a first impression!

It is still very important that you create the right impression as soon as you walk into the room. Walking in to the interview you will naturally feel nervous, everybody does.

Whilst some scope for your nerves will be taken into account during the interview, remember that the role you are applying for is one that requires confidence, self belief and the ability to work well under pressure. On the following pages we have provided you with a number of tips and advice to help you make a good first impression at the interview.

TIPS FOR CREATING A GOOD FIRST IMPRESSION

TIP 1 – STAND TALL

When you walk into the room, make sure you are standing tall. Sometimes you will see people who are taller than they actually look. The reason for this is that their posture is not correct and they are slouching or leaning forward. Stand in front of the mirror, push your chest out and lift your head up. Unless you have perfect posture you should see your height increase slightly. The other added benefit of standing tall is that you will be able to breathe far easier. Standing tall allows the rib cage to open and your lungs to expand to their full capacity. This, in turn, will increase your confidence.

TIP 2 – SMILE… Very important!

When you travel with any tour operator you should be able to notice that the holiday reps are generally upbeat and smiling. Smiling is contagious and shows a warm side to your personality. Whilst you should be careful not to overdo it, you must try to smile often during your interview. It will help you, and the panel, to relax, thus ensuring you perform to the best of your ability.

TIP 3 – COMMUNICATE EFFECTIVELY

Do you know anybody who likes the sound of their own voice? Are they good at listening too? There are a number of elements to effective communication. Two of these are talking and listening. Having the ability to know the 'right' moment to talk is important. Whilst the interview is about the panel getting to know you and your capabilities, it is also an opportunity for them to look at other areas including your personality, presence, appearance and communication skills. Don't overtake the interview by talking too much and,

certainly, do not talk over any of the panel. When the panel are talking, listen carefully. Nod, confirm and agree where appropriate. Also try to use appropriate facial expressions, too. This will show the panel that you are capable of listening to customers' complaints and concerns, which is a big part of a holiday rep's role.

TIP 4 – SIT UPRIGHT

When you are invited to sit down, make sure you sit upright in the chair. Once again, creating a good, positive posture has many benefits, as previously stated. Place your hands on your knees and relax – remember to smile.

Many people like using their hands to express themselves when answering interview questions. Whilst this is ok to do, make sure you don't overuse them, as this can detract from your responses and will become irritating to the panel.

TIP 5 – ASK RELEVANT QUESTIONS ONLY

At the end of the interview, you will be given the opportunity to ask questions.

We recommend that you have two questions to ask the panel, but remember the following advice: Don't try to be clever and ask technical or complicated questions that could catch out the panel.

Don't ask questions relating to pay, holidays or leave.

Ask questions that show you are interested in the tour operator and their future ambitions, or the opportunities for development. At the end of this section, we have provided you with a number of useful questions to ask the panel.

To watch free videos on how to improve your interview technique search for 'how2become' on YouTube.com.

RESEARCH

Of course, no company expects you to know everything about them before you start working for them, but you will be expected to know certain facts. This is where you have the opportunity to demonstrate to the panel that you have done your homework. It is important that you show a keen interest in the service and that you have researched their company to the best of your ability. You will want to visit their website and write down facts about their company policies, where they fly to, their achievements and future goals and aspirations.

The tour operator website should have information about customer care/relations which you should read thoroughly so that you understand the type of service they offer. Who are the board members and what is the role of a holiday rep with this particular tour operator?

It is also worth trying to obtain literature about the company and you may be able to get a friend or relative to write to them asking for any company information which may help you in your preparation.

Here is a research checklist to help make sure you cover each important topic.

TOUR OPERATOR RESEARCH CHECKLIST

- What is the tour operator's mission statement?
- Where do they fly to?
- Are there any future plans for expansion or growth?
- Who are the tour operator's major competitors?
- How many employees do they have at any one time?
- What products and services do they offer?

- What do you like about this particular tour operator?

- What is the tour operator's customer care policy?

- How long have they been operating?

QUESTIONS AND SAMPLE RESPONSES

Now we will take a look at the possible interview questions you will be asked to answer on the actual day. Within this part of the guide we have provided you with a number of the more common interview questions used by tour operators. Please remember that they are to be used as a guide only and are not guaranteed to be the actual questions that you will be asked on the day.

Following each question we have provided you with an explanation as to what the panel are looking for from the candidate. Then we have supplied a sample response to each question, to help you structure your own individual response. During the interview, you may find that some questions are repeated from the application form. If this is the case, make sure you use a different response to the ones you put down on the application form. This allows you to demonstrate that you have a wider experience base in each area duplicated.

QUESTION NUMBER 1

Why do you want to become a holiday rep?

You will, most probably, have already answered this question when completing the application form. If this is the case, have a look at your application form response prior to the interview to make sure you give an alternative answer and also that you do not contradict yourself the second time around. When answering this question, concentrate on covering the following elements:

- The main reason why – your ambition.

- The suitability of your personal qualities and attributes.

- The positive aspects of the role – variety, flexibility, working with others, etc.

- Helping others/Customer care, etc.

We have now provided you with a sample response to this type of question.

Once you have read our response use it to construct your own using a blank sheet of paper.

SAMPLE RESPONSE

Why do you want to become a holiday rep?

"This is something that I have always wanted to do. Ever since I went on holiday as a child, I have aspired to a member of a holiday rep team. Although I enjoy my current job, I would now like a career that is more challenging, varied and exciting. I believe my own personal qualities would suit the role of a holiday rep and I get great satisfaction from working in a team environment, where everybody is working towards the same

goal. I understand that delivering a high level of service to the customer is a priority in this industry, and this is something that I would enjoy doing."

KEY AREAS TO CONSIDER:

- The main reason for wanting to become a holiday rep.

- The positive aspects of the job.

- Working in a team environment.

- Providing a high standard of customer care.

QUESTION NUMBER 2

Why do you want to work for our tour operator?

Once again, you may have already answered this question during the application form stage. If this is the case, remember to check your answer first before attending the interview. When answering this question, you must be positive about their tour operator. The main reason for the panel asking this question is that they want to know you have researched them thoroughly, and that you are serious about wanting to join them.

Many candidates apply for many different tour operators just because they want to become a holiday rep. Wanting to join their particular tour operator is just as important as wanting to become a holiday rep.

When answering this type of question, try to cover the following areas:

- Their reputation (providing it is positive).

- The quality of their product.

- The tour operator's ambitions and achievements.

- What they stand for.

This type of question allows you really show that you have researched this particular tour company and that you are dedicated to becoming a rep with them. If the assessors can start to see you as part of their team your chances of success will be greatly increased. If you provide a response that is not specific to their company then this highlights that you have not prepared for the assessment day and this is not someone they will want to take on. Now, take a look at the sample response before creating your own using a blank sheet of paper.

SAMPLE RESPONSE

Why do you want to work for our tour operator?

"Prior to attending the selection process, I researched a number of different tour operators before deciding to apply for yours. I was impressed by the quality of service the tour operator offers and I already know that it has an excellent reputation.

Your customer service standards are high and the quality of training given to holiday reps is exceptional. Having spoken to some of your existing employees, all of them were very happy in their work and stated that you are a very good employer.

You are an exciting tour operator that has achieved much to date and I like the fact that you are always looking for innovative ways to improve and develop.

I would like to work for a tour operator that cares about its customers, which you do. If the customer is happy and their experience of staying with you is a good one, they are likely

to come back again. I would love to be a part of this team and believe the qualities I have will help it to continue to move forward and stay ahead of its competitors."

KEY AREAS TO CONSIDER:

- The tour operator's reputation.
- The quality of their product and what they stand for.
- The tour operator's ambitions and achievements.

QUESTION NUMBER 3

What makes you better than the next candidate and, therefore, why should we offer you the position?

This is another opportunity for you to sell yourself. This is quite a common question during interviews and the way you approach it should be in a positive manner. The question is designed to assess your confidence and determine the type of qualities you have. Don't fall into the trap of answering this question in the same way that the majority of people do.

Many people will reply with a response along the following line:

"I am the best person for the job because this is something that I've always wanted to do. I am a hard worker who is enthusiastic and determined to be successful."

This type of response is not factual or unique in content. Try to focus your response on the job and how best you match it. The tour operator want to know that they'll look back in a years' time and think that they are glad they employed you.

SAMPLE RESPONSE

What makes you better than the next candidate and, therefore, why should we offer you the position?

"I have researched both the role that I am applying for, and your tour operator. Looking at the required skills of the role and the type of person you are looking for, I believe I am the best person for the job. I have a proven track record in delivering a high level of customer service and have experience in dealing with customer complaints. I have been on a number of training courses before and always ensure that I put in the required amount of work to successfully pass them to a high standard.

I am a confident and reliable person who works very well in a team environment. In my previous role as a restaurant manager, I often had to work to tight schedules and always remained calm when under pressure. Finally, my personal circumstances are extremely flexible and, having studied the role of a holiday rep, I understand the obligations and requirements in terms of availability.

If successful, I promise that I won't let you down and I will work hard to make sure that I live up to expectations of the tour operator."

KEY AREAS TO CONSIDER:

- Your previous experience and how it relates to the role.

- Be positive, confident and upbeat in your response.

- Cover the key qualities and attributes and match them with your own experience.

QUESTION NUMBER 4

What are your weaknesses and what do you need to work on?

This is a classic interview question and can be quite difficult to answer for many people. Those people who say they have no weaknesses are not telling the truth. We all have areas that we can improve on, but you need to be careful what you disclose when responding to this type of question. For example, if you tell the panel that you are an awful time keeper you might as well leave the interview there and then! They will admire your honesty, but the role requires people who are punctual and are not going to be late for work. The best way to prepare for this type of question is to write down all of your weaknesses. Once you have done that, pick one that you can turn into a positive.

Take a look at the sample response we have provided and see how we have turned the weakness around to our advantage. Once you have read the response, use a blank sheet of paper to prepare your own response based on your own circumstances.

SAMPLE RESPONSE

What are your weaknesses and what do you need to work on?

"That's a difficult question to answer but I am aware of a weakness that I have.

I tend to set myself high standards both personally and professionally. The problem is, I sometimes expect it from other people, too. For example, I find it difficult to accept it when people are late for an appointment that we have agreed. In those situations, I need to learn to let it go over my head and just accept that everybody is different."

KEY AREAS TO CONSIDER:

- Be honest, but don't talk about any weaknesses you may have that are in relation to the job description.

- Turn your weakness into a positive.

- Say that you are working on your weakness.

- If you really cannot think of a weakness, tell them about one that you used to have.

QUESTION NUMBER 5

Describe a situation at work where you have had to be flexible.

Part of the holiday rep's role is to be flexible. Part of the essential criteria for becoming a holiday rep is that you are flexible. This means that you are flexible in terms of the roster and your availability. In order for the tour operator to operate effectively, it needs people who do not want to work a normal 9 – 5 job. You may have to be at the airport for 3am in order to pick up guests at 5am. Are you flexible enough to do this?

Many holiday reps say that the most frustrating aspect of their job is the instability of the life and the roster changes. Obviously the tour operator wants to know that this is not going to be a problem for you. Therefore, when responding to this type of question, you need to provide an example where you have already demonstrated commitment and flexibility to a previous or current role.

Read the sample response we have provided before using a blank sheet of paper to create your own response.

SAMPLE REPSONSE

Describe a situation at work where you have had to be flexible.

"Whilst working in my current role as a hairdresser, I was asked by my employer to work late every Saturday evening. The reason for this was that a number of clients could only make appointments between 6pm and 8pm on Saturday evenings. Although I usually go out on a Saturday night, I decided to agree to the additional hours. The salon was doing well and was beginning to get a very good reputation. I wanted to help the salon provide a high level of service to its customers and understood that if I didn't work late on those evenings they would lose the custom.

Fortunately, 2 months on, another member of the team has volunteered to help me cover the Saturday evenings, so I now only have to work every other Saturday. I fully understand that holiday reps need to be flexible in terms of their roster and working hours. My personal life would allow for this and I believe it is a small sacrifice to pay for such a rewarding career. I can be relied upon to be flexible when required."

KEY AREAS TO CONSIDER:

- Demonstrate that your personal circumstances allow for flexibility.

- Provide an example where you have gone out of your way to help your employer. Tell them that you understand how important flexible working is to the role of a holiday rep.

QUESTION NUMBER 6

What challenges will our tour operator face in the future and how could you, as a holiday rep, help us to overcome these?

This type of question serves two main purposes for the panel. The first purpose is that it assesses how much you understand about the tour operator industry, in terms of its competitiveness. The second purpose is that it assesses your awareness of how influential holiday reps are in their role.

Holiday reps are some of the most important employees of a tour operator. If customers have a bad experience whilst on holiday then they are unlikely to return to that tour operator. There are so many different tour operators to choose from and competition is fierce, so staying ahead of the game and providing an exceptional level of service is important. It is so important that the holiday rep staff are friendly, helpful and customer focused.

SAMPLE RESPONSE

What challenges will our tour operator face in the future and how could you, as a holiday rep, help us to overcome these?

"The travel industry is extremely competitive and the expectations of the customer are always on the increase. People generally want to pay less for their service but still expect a high level of customer care. In addition to the competitiveness of the modern day market, there is also the issue of security and the financial implications this has in terms of additional training and advanced security measures. The cost of fuel and salary expenses will continue to increase, which will undoubtedly have an effect on the cost of the product.

Therefore, it is important that holiday reps provide the highest level of customer service at all times. Ensuring the customer is satisfied with the service will mean they are far more likely to come back to the tour operator time and time again. More importantly however, they will recommend the tour company to their friends and relatives."

KEY AREAS TO CONSIDER:

- Competitiveness of the industry, security issues and increased operating costs for the tour operator.

- High customer expectations and how holiday rep can help deliver this.

- A quality service means customers are far more likely to return and use the service again.

QUESTION NUMBER 7

Do you think you will find the change of lifestyle difficult to adapt to if you are successful in becoming a holiday rep?

There is only one answer to this question and that is 'No, it will not be difficult to adapt to'. When answering questions of this nature, tell them that you have researched the role and are fully aware of the implications, including the change of lifestyle it will bring.

Also, remember to touch on the specifics about the change in lifestyle, what it means to you and how you have prepared for it. Don't be afraid to say that some areas will be a challenge for you, but that you are fully committed and prepared for everything the job presents.

SAMPLE RESPONSE

Do you think you will find the change of lifestyle difficult to adapt to if you are successful in becoming a holiday rep?

"Although this is something that I have dreamt of doing for many years now, I have still taken the time to look into the lifestyle change and how it will affect me. Whilst some areas will be challenging, I am 100% confident I will not have any problems adapting.

My personal circumstances are such that I can work the roster system comfortably and I am prepared for being away from home for long periods, as and when required. I have few personal commitments at home and am fully prepared for the lifestyle change, if I am successful in my application.

In fact, I am very much looking forward to the change, as it is something I have wanted for a long time. I live life to the full and my personality is one that is adaptable to most circumstances."

KEY AREAS TO CONSIDER:

- Smile and be enthusiastic in your response.

- Talk about the change in lifestyle for you and how you have prepared for it.

- You have thought long and hard about this career and your personal circumstances are suited to the role.

QUESTION NUMBER 8

How would you deal with somebody in a work situation who you felt was not pulling their weight and working as part of the team?

This type of question can be asked in a variety of formats. You may be asked to provide an example of where you have dealt with this type of situation in your current or previous role. The question is designed to assess your assertiveness and confidence, whilst being tactful. They are not looking for you to respond in a confrontational manner but, instead, looking for you to approach the person and resolve the issue with the minimum of fuss. To ignore the issue is not an option.

We have now provided a response which gives an example of a work situation. Somebody is taking too many breaks and not pulling weight. Once you have read the example, try to think of any experiences you have where you have had to deal with this type of issue. Then, use a blank sheet of paper to create a response.

SAMPLE RESONSE

How would you deal with somebody in a work situation who you felt was not pulling their weight and working as part of the team?

"Whilst working in my current role as a waiter for a local restaurant, I was aware of a colleague who was taking more breaks than he was entitled to.

Whilst he was taking these additional breaks, the rest of the team would have to cover for the shortfall. Unfortunately, the customer would then suffer as the time it took for them to be served would increase.

I decided to approach the person in order to resolve the issue. I walked over to him and asked him in a friendly manner if he

would come and help the rest of team serve the customers. I told him that we were busy and that we needed his help.

Fortunately, he responded in a positive manner and realised that he was taking advantage of his rest periods. Since then, there has not been an issue. It is important that the team gets on and works well together. We cannot afford to have confrontational situations and the best way to resolve issues like this is to be honest and tactful."

KEY AREAS TO CONSIDER:

- Do not be confrontational.

- Be tactful in your approach, focusing on the customer as the priority.

- Effective teamwork is essential.

- Do not ignore the situation, but instead deal with it tactfully.

QUESTION NUMBER 9

How do you feel about working with people from different cultures and backgrounds?

This is quite a common interview question and one that you need to be prepared for. Respect for diversity is essential to the role of a holiday rep. You will be working with both colleagues and customers from different cultures and backgrounds and, therefore, it is important that you are comfortable with this. We live in a diverse community that brings many positive aspects that we can learn from. When answering the question, you should be aiming to demonstrate that you are totally at ease when working with people from different cultures and backgrounds.

Take a look at the response on the following page before using a blank sheet of paper to construct your own answer to this type of question.

Remember to be honest in your reply and only state the facts about your feelings towards people from different cultures. If you are not truthful in your response, you will not be doing yourself, or the tour operator, any favours.

SAMPLE RESPONSE

How do you feel about working with people from different cultures and backgrounds?

"I am totally at ease in those situations, in fact I don't even think about it. This has never been a problem for me. I have a sincere interest in people from different cultures and backgrounds and have learnt many things from them in the past. I would like to think that we can all learn something from everybody, regardless of their culture or background and this is a part of the job that I would look forward to.

There are so many different and exciting things to learn in life and this can only be achieved by meeting, respecting and understanding people from different cultures and backgrounds. Teams that are diverse in nature have a better chance of delivering a higher quality of service. If the customer base is diverse, then so should the workforce that delivers the service."

KEY AREAS TO CONSIDER:

- Be honest when answering this type of question.

- Demonstrate that you understand diversity and the benefits this brings to society. Provide examples where appropriate.

QUESTION NUMBER 10

What is the best example of customer service that you have come across?

What is the best example of customer service that you have come across?

The majority of tour operators pride themselves on their high level of service. However, some are better than others.

This type of question is designed to see how high your standards are, in relation to customer service. Those people who have a great deal of experience in a customer-focused environment will be able to answer this question with relative ease.

However, those who have little experience in this area will need to spend more time preparing their response. Try to think of an occasion when you have witnessed an excellent piece of customer service and show that you learned from it. If you are very confident, then you may have an occasion when you, yourself, provided that service. Whatever response you provide, make sure it is unique and stands out.

SAMPLE RESPONSE

What is the best example of customer service that you have come across?

"Whilst working as a shop assistant in my current role, a member of the public came in to complain to the manager about a pair of football shoes that he had bought for his son's birthday. When his son came to open the present on the morning of his birthday, he noticed that one of the football boots was a larger size than the other. He was supposed to be playing football with his friends that morning and wanted

to wear his new boots. However, due to the shop's mistake, this was not possible. Naturally, the boy was very upset.

The manager of the shop was excellent in her approach to dealing with situation. She remained calm throughout and listened to the gentleman very carefully, showing complete empathy for his son's situation. This immediately defused any potential confrontation. She then told him how sorry she was for the mistake that had happened, and that she would feel exactly the same if it was her own son who it had happened to. She then told the gentleman that she would refund the money in full and give his son a new pair of football boots to the same value as the previous pair.

The man was delighted with her offer. Not only that, she then offered to give the man a further discount of 10% on any future purchase, due to the added inconvenience that was caused by him having to return to the shop to sort out the problem. I learned a lot from the way my manager dealt with this situation. She used exceptional communication skills and remained calm throughout. She then went the extra mile to make the gentleman's journey back to the shop a worthwhile one.

The potential for losing a customer was averted by her actions and I feel sure the man would return to our shop again."

KEY AREAS TO CONSIDER:

- Use an example where somebody has gone the extra mile.

- Remember that part of the role of a holiday rep is to provide a high level of customer service.

- Tell them what you learned from the experience.

QUESTION NUMBER 11

What do you think makes a successful holiday rep team?

Part of the role of a holiday rep is to be a competent and effective team player. The purpose of this question is to assess your knowledge of what a team is and how it operates effectively. Some of the important aspects to remember, when operating as a holiday rep team member, are as follows:

- Gets on well with the rest of the team.

- Offers effective solutions to problem solving.

- Utilises effective listening skills both verbal and non-verbal.

- Makes an effort to involve others.

- Can be adaptable and willing to try others' ideas.

- Gives positive feedback to the rest of the team.

- When things are going wrong, remains positive and enthusiastic.

These are just a few examples of how a member of a team can help contribute in a positive way.

SAMPLE RESPONSE

What do you think makes a successful holiday rep team?

"There are a number of important elements that would make a successful holiday rep team. To begin with, it is important to have different types of people in terms of their personalities, views and opinions. This way you are more likely to get a variety of options and solutions to problems when they arise.

The team members need to be positive, enthusiastic and have the ability to get

on with each other. There should be no confrontation between members of the team and an understanding from everyone that they are working together to achieve a common goal of delivering a high quality service, and also ensuring the safety of all passengers.

Each member of the team should be a competent communicator and be able to listen to other people's ideas and opinions. Flexibility in the team is also important to try new and different ideas when appropriate. Every team member should provide encouragement and work hard together when the pressure is on. Above all, holiday reps are role models for the tour operator, and each member of the team should uphold the values of their employer."

KEY AREAS TO CONSIDER:

- Utilise key words in your response.

- Demonstrate that you understand the qualities of an effective team.

- Remember the ultimate aim of delivering a high quality service and ensuring the safety of all passengers.

QUESTION NUMBER 12

If you were not successful today would you re-apply?

If you are not successful today, would you re-apply? There is only one answer to this type of question and that is "Yes I would". The question is designed to see how dedicated you are to their particular tour operator. The important thing to remember, when responding to this type of question, is to mention that you would look to improve on your weak areas for next time.

Determination is the key to success and if you are not accepted the first time, you will work hard to improve for the next time. Most people, if asked this question, think they have failed and are not going to be offered a job. Do not fall into this trap. It is a question that is designed to see how committed you are to joining their tour operator! Be positive in your response.

SAMPLE RESONSE

If you were not successful today would you re-apply?

'Yes I would, most definitely. I have researched many different tour operators and this is the one that I would like to join. If I am not successful at this attempt, then I will go away and look for ways to improve. Whilst I would be disappointed, I would not be negative about the situation.

One of my qualities is that I have the ability to accept, and work on, my weaknesses. If there was the option for feedback, I would take this up and improve on the areas I needed to work on. However, I would love to be successful at this attempt and do believe that I am ready, now, to become a competent and professional holiday rep with your tour operator.'

KEY AREAS TO CONSIDER:

- The only real answer to this question is 'yes'.

- Be positive about the prospect of not being successful and tell them that you would work on your weaknesses.

- Don't be afraid to be confident in your own abilities.

QUESTION NUMBER 13

How many times have you called in sick within the last year?

This is an easy question to answer, but one that can do you some damage if you have a poor sickness record.

The ideal answer here is zero days. The tour operator need people who are reliable. If a member of the holiday rep team calls in sick on the day their customers arrive, this will cause problems for the tour operator. They then have to dedicate time and resources to phone around and find somebody else to cover for the sick person. Genuine sickness cannot be avoided. However, in every job there are people who take advantage of sick leave, which costs employees thousands of pounds every year. The tour operator industry is keen to avoid employing people who have a poor sickness record.

SAMPLE RESONSE

How many times have you called in sick within the last year?

'I have had no days off sick within the last 12 months. I am an honest person and would only ever call in sick if I really could not make it to work. I understand that the tour operator needs to employ reliable people and if a member of the team goes sick, you will need to find somebody else to cover for them.'

KEY AREAS TO CONSIDER:

- The least day's sickness you have, the better.

- Be aware of the implications for the tour operator if an employee is constantly calling in sick.

- Genuine sickness cannot be avoided.

PREPARATION CHECKLIST 10 POINT ACTION PLAN

1 Decide on the type of rep you want to become

2 Research the tour operator/s that best suits the rep you want to become

3 Print off / download the application form, prepare your application form and the apply your tour operator/s

4 Read the letter from the tour operator carefully so you know exactly what to prepare for you assessment day

5 Prepare you introduction

6 Prepare you presentation

7 Prepare for your maths and brochure test

8 Prepare for your roleplays

9 Prepare for you group exercises

10 Prepare for you one on one interview

What Next?

At this point, you will have hopefully passed the assessment day and the interview and been offered a job. This may be on the same day, the next day or a week after it all depends on the tour operator. You will then receive your contract and details of your placement. If you have passed the interview stage then you are nearly there; all it is now is the training course.

Training courses can run between 1 week and 4 weeks, depending on tour operator. The days are long and will involve intense training to prepare you for your role as a holiday rep. The training course days usually start between 8 am and 9 am and finish between 6pm and 7pm. After the training day has finished the evening entertainment will often include various team building exercises followed by opportunities go out and explore the local town. However, you must be aware that the following day will often include exams and presentations and that even though you have come this far it is still possible to be removed from the training course.

You are still being watched and assessed and after all the hard work you have put in getting sent home is the last thing you want.

HINTS AND TIPS TO REMEMBER

- Make sure you are constantly SMILING during your assessment day, even if you make mistakes this can sometimes be the deciding factor!

- Try as much as you can to enjoy the whole experience from your assessment day to the training course to the resort induction. It is a once in the life time opportunity so enjoy the whole experience

- When preparing for your brochure test if you have missed your opportunity to visit your local travel agent check to see if you can download the brochures from the tour operators website.

- Once you have become a holiday rep remember to buy local brands of food at the supermarkets as the major brands in the UK are normally imported and cost more.

- Try to build a relationship with your local restaurant and bar managers as they will often give you a discount on food and drinks if you recommend them to your customers. It is good advertisement for them to have a holiday rep eating/ drinking in their establishment

- Take things with you that remind you of home. For example many reps take their own bed sheets and pillow cases .

- Always try to find out the reason for your customer being on holiday. For example they could have come away for their birthday. In this case a card and drink goes a long to delivering that extra bit of customer service!

- Try and keep a daily record of events. This will help you to keep track of your sales and commission each week, any problems with any guests, any problems with any properties and your progress as a holiday rep.

CHAPTER SEVEN

TOUR OPERATOR CONTACT DETAILS

Within this section of the guide we have provided tour operator contact details to make it easier for you to research and apply. The majority of tour operators provide recruitment information through their websites. When researching the role of both a holiday rep and the tour operator, your first port of call should be the website. This will provide you with plenty of up–to-date information about the tour operator, its products and service, possible future developments and how they operate. Take a piece of paper and a pen, and then spend some time studying the website of your chosen tour operator. Write down any information that will help you during your application.

You will also find that many tour operators allow you to apply online through their online application form. If this is

the case, remember to print off your completed form before submitting it. You will need to make reference to it prior to the assessment centre. Make sure to check that you meet the minimum requirements, of the tour operator you wish to apply for, before submitting your application form – many of them vary.

HOLIDAY REP CONTACT DETAILS

CLUB 18-30
www.club18-30.com

COSMOS
www.cosmos-holidays.co.uk

CRYSTAL HOLIDAYS
www.crystalholidays.co.uk

ESPRIT
www.esprit-holidays.co.uk
www.skijob.co.uk

EURO CAMP
www.eurocamp.co.uk
www.holidaybreakjobs.com

FIRST CHOICE
www.firstchoice.co.uk
www.tuitraveljobs.co.uk

KUONI
www.kuoni.co.uk

MY TRAVEL
www.mytravel.com

OLYMPIC HOLIDAYS
www.olympicholidays.com

THOMAS COOK
www.thomascook.com

THOMSON
www.thomson.co.uk

ADDITION CONTACT DETAILS

Association of British Travel Agents (ABTA)
68-71 Newman Street, London W1T 3AH
Tel: 020 7637 2444
www.abta.com

Association of Independent Tour Operators (AITO)
133a St Margaret's Road, Twickenham TW1 1RG
Tel: 020 8744 9280
www.aito.co.uk

Institute of Travel and Tourism (ITT)
PO Box 217, Ware, Herts SG12 8WY
Tel: 0870 770 7960
www.itt.co.uk

The Tourism Society
Trinity Court, 34 West Street, Sutton, Surrey SM1 1SH
Tel: 020 8661 4636
www.tourismsociety.org

how2become

Visit www.how2become.com to find
more titles and courses that will
help you to pass any job interview or
selection process:

- Online testing suite and videos

- Job interview DVDs and books

- 1-day intensive career training courses

- Psychometric testing books and CDs.

www.how2become.com